Mary at the Crossroads of History

Rev. Francis J. Hoffman, JCD

RELEVANT RADIO®
2020

To St. Joseph, Protector of the Universal Church.

Contents

Foreword: The Inflection Point..1

1. The Millennium Game...3

2. In the Beginning..9

3. Mother of God, Mother of the Church...............................25

4. The Confrontation in Spain...37

5. The Flowering of Christendom..49

6. Meeting of the Worlds..63

7. The Battle for Christendom...81

8. The Century of Fatima.,,..87

9. The Battle for Life—and Relevant Radio's Part in It............95

10. What We Can Do—with Our Lady's Help.........................105

Some Sources..119

About the Author...120

About Relevant Radio...121

Foreword: The Inflection Point

The idea for this book began on December 31, 1999, while driving across Nebraska. But now, twenty years later, we're at an inflection point in history, and it is time to write this book.

If you're mathematically inclined, you may actually remember hearing about "inflection points" in calculus class. In calculus, an inflection point is the point where a curve changes from convex to concave.

So an inflection point in history is a point where things are about to change—for the better or for the worse. An inflection point is a point where *we can do something* to change history.

And I'm about to tell you a little secret that not very many people know:

We're *always* at an inflection point in history.

Remember what Charles Dickens wrote at the beginning of *A Tale of Two Cities*, a love story set in the drama of the French Revolution?

> It was the best of times, it was the worst of times, it was the age of wisdom, it was the age of foolishness, it was the epoch of belief, it was the epoch of incredulity, it was the season of Light, it was the season of Darkness, it was the spring of hope, it was the winter of despair, we had everything before us, we had nothing before us, we were all going direct to Heaven, we were all going direct the other way—in short, the period was so far like the present period, that some of its noisiest authorities insisted on its being received, for good or for evil, in the superlative degree of comparison only.

Dickens knew what he was talking about. It was a time where everything hung in the balance. It was a time where things could go either way.

It was a time, he said, just like today.

And that's because *every* time is a time just like today. We're *always* at a point where things could change completely. We're always at a point where things could get very much better or very much worse.

We're human beings, made in the image of God. We have free will.

But the question is, what will we do with it?

Adam and Eve, our first parents, had free will, and they used it to rebel against God. They could choose to do God's will, or they could choose to be persuaded by the serpent. They chose the serpent—a choice that meant death and exile from Paradise.

We can make that choice every day. Every day, we have to face the same decision: God's way or the serpent's? You and I are always at an inflection point in history, but only if we decide to act and do something about it. Filled with hope, we who are the children of God do act, because we are convinced that with God's grace everything can change for the better in an instant.

But also every day, we *could* do what Adam and Eve did. We could decide that we want things our own way—which is Satan's way.

But we don't have to do it that way. There's another model we could follow.

Her words echo down through history, and they change everything:

"Behold, I am the handmaid of the Lord. May it be done to me according to your word."

That is the real inflection point in history. That is the point that divides everything into before and after. That is the moment when B.C. (before Christ) becomes A.D., *anno Domini*, in the Year of the Lord. And the rest of this book is all about how everything changed, *and can still change*, because one woman had the faith and the courage to say, "May it be done to me according to your word."

1. The Millennium Game

Where were you on December 31, 1999? As I wrote a few pages ago, the idea for this book began in the afternoon of December 31, 1999, while driving across Nebraska.

If you were old enough to remember it at all, you remember that date. It was Y2K, and you were probably a bit apprehensive about what might happen to the power grid in America when the clock struck midnight January 1, 2000.

Everyone was concerned about Y2K. Some people were convinced that the world was going to end. (There were people who were convinced the world was going to end at Y1K, too, and by the way they were wrong.)

Other people were convinced that it was just going to be a big fat mess. You remember the Y2K bug. For years, people had been entering dates in computer databases with only two digits for the year—like 72 for 1972, or 87 for 1987. In the early days of computers, it made sense. Memory was expensive, and you didn't have much of it. If you cut off two digits from the year, you saved two whole bytes of memory. It sounds like a ridiculously small number to worry about now, but my first computer had 16 kilobytes of memory. In a list of dates, saving 2 bytes per date was a big deal. And anyway, who expected those computers to last more than a few years?

But they did last, because they worked. In 1999, many banks and insurance companies were still using big mainframe computers from the 1960s, because upgrading would be expensive, and you don't mess with a system that works. But suddenly they were really scared. What would happen to everyone's investments when the year rolled around to 2000, and the computer thought it was 99 years *before* 1999?

Not the first time humanity got in trouble by not thinking ahead.

I know people who stockpiled bottled water because they were absolutely convinced that, for some reason, the Y2K bug would turn off all the valves at the waterworks. There were preppers with basements full of canned food. Generator salesmen were buying themselves Cadillacs.

So practically everybody I knew had seen scare stories in the media about Y2K. And practically everybody I knew asked me, "Father Rocky, where are *you* going to be on December 31, 1999?"

And I said, "I'll probably be on my way back from a father-son ski trip in Colorado. Because I don't care if the world's going to end. I wanna go skiing."

Then they would look at me as if I'd lost my mind, so I'd have to add, "The kids want to go skiing, too." That made it all right. I was doing it for the kids.

Surviving Nebraska

So that's where I was—on my way back from a father-son ski trip. Back when I was chaplain at Northridge Prep in Chicago, we did this every year: we'd take the fathers and sons out to camp at Ski Eldora, and it was a great time. But our schedule put us on the road on December 31, with the year 2000 just hours away.

You can imagine the scene, because there's not much to imagine. We're in Nebraska on route 80. It's a long trip. There's nothing to see. I mean, you never saw so much nothing. It's flat, and there are fields, and in the winter those fields aren't growing much. Sometimes you see a town in the distance, and usually a town means some houses and a gas station and nothing else.

Mostly what you see is road.

It's the kind of road where you can drive ninety miles an hour and still get nowhere. Off to the left is the River Platte, a mile wide and an inch deep. The Transcontinental Railroad runs alongside, too, and that's interesting to talk about for maybe five minutes.

It's a long trip with teenage boys—fourteen, fifteen, sixteen years old. I could feel the boredom in the stale air.

So somewhere around Ogallala I said—and I don't know if it was an inspiration or what, but this is what I said—"Hey, let's play the Millennium Game!"

I was desperate to distract the boys. But I hadn't really thought through what I'd say next.

Naturally, they asked, "What's the Millennium Game?"

I had to think of something quickly, so I said, "Well, you can only play it once every thousand years, and tonight's the night. It's the last day of the millennium."

"Well, how do you play it?" they asked.

A very good question.

Now I had to make something up. "So here's what we do: we go around the circle, and everybody proposes what was the most important event in human history in that thousand years, and then you have to defend it."

I was surprised, and relieved, when the boys seemed to think it was a good idea. But I began to wonder after the first round. We hardly used up any miles on that one, because everyone agreed: the most important event of the first millennium A.D. was the birth of Christ. There was no discussion about that at all.

All right, let's go to the second round. And here was where it turned out to be really fascinating. I started to learn how well-educated these boys were and how well they understood history.

The second millennium

The first boy said, "Hmm... The most important event of the last thousand years, from 1000 A.D. to 2000 A.D., was the invention of the printing press."

"I see. And why do you say that?"

"Because now you can spread knowledge much more quickly. Information goes everywhere. People can share research, do science, spread ideas in a way they never could before."

Well, he certainly had a point there. Think how many amazing things have happened because we have books and magazines and newspapers—all thanks to Johann Gutenberg and his printing press. And what was the first book he printed? The Bible, naturally. So a machine that made it possible for every family to have a Bible certainly changed the world. I had to agree: the invention of printing was a big, important event.

That used up some miles.

But the game certainly wasn't over yet, because as we were passing North Platte, the next boy said, "No, I think it was the harnessing of electricity with Thomas Edison. In fact, he may have been the most important person in the last thousand years. Think of all the things we have because he encouraged us to use electricity. Electric lights, of course, and radios, and television, and computers, and refrigerators..."

Well, that was pretty good. I had to agree, practical electricity changed the world. And, just for the sake of keeping the game simple, I didn't argue about whether you should give Edison or Westinghouse or Tesla the credit for electricity. It was enough to say that electricity changed the world. It got us to about Gothenburg, anyway.

We kept going. Another thought it was the invention of nuclear power, and we talked about that to Lexington or so. Another thought it was the Internet. That was a good one—it got us almost to Grand Island.

And then finally one of the boys said, "No, I think the most important event of the last thousand years was the apparition of the Blessed Mother to Juan Diego at Tepeyac Hill on December 12, 1531."

It hit me hard—so hard that I was pretty sure we had a winner here. I didn't even know what the rules of the Millennium Game were, but I was pretty sure this guy had won it.

But still, I wanted to be scrupulously fair and play by the rules, even if I was making them up as I went along. So I said, "Good. Now please defend that. Why do you say that was the most important event?"

"It had to be," he answered. "Take a look. One thousand years ago—the year 1000 A.D.—from north to south, in the Western Hemisphere as we understand it, there was not one single Christian. In the year 2000, in the Western Hemisphere, from the north to the south, the vast majority of people are baptized Christians—in Canada, the United States, Mexico, Central America, South America. Millions and millions of people became Christians because Our Lady appeared to Juan Diego. I can't think of *anything* that changed the world more than that in the last thousand years."

He won the day. I didn't even have to make up a rule for how you win the game, because everyone agreed that he had won.

Think of it. The most important event in the last thousand years! It couldn't be anything else, now that I'd thought about it. I mean, you take a look at the megatrends of how history moves, the significant changes on the world map. That young man made the best case.

And there she is: Mary at the crossroads of history. Because there are inflection points in human history, aren't there? There are points where history has been going one way and then changes to another way, and you can see that the transition point was one event. And I'm going to make a bold assertion right here: I think every time you come to a truly world-changing event, you'll find Mary right there.

Don't believe me? That's good. If you agreed with me right away, there wouldn't be any need for the rest of this book. But now you know what the title means, anyway.

And now I have to make my case. I have to show you that Mary really does stand at the crossroads of history, every time history comes to a crossroads.

Think I can do it? Let's find out. We'll start right at the beginning.

2. In the Beginning

Did you know that the man who came up with the "big bang" theory was a Catholic priest?

His name was Georges Henri Joseph Édouard Lemaître, and he was a Jesuit from Belgium (where people seem to have a lot of names). You probably know that Jesuits have to go through a lot of education. It's their thing. So most Jesuits are pretty smart, and Fr. Lemaître was smarter than the average Jesuit.

Back in the 1920s, almost every scientist thought the universe had always existed and always would exist in pretty much a steady state. The idea that it actually *began* at some point—well, that was religion, wasn't it? If the world was created, that meant a creator.

But Fr. Lemaître wasn't blinded by scientistic prejudice. He just looked at the evidence. And the evidence was coming in from all over: the whole universe seemed to be expanding from a single point. It was logical to conclude, then, that everything had started at that one point. The whole universe must have begun as a "primeval atom," and suddenly begun expanding with unimaginable force.

Most scientists rejected the idea—at first. One of the steady-staters called this theory the "big bang," and the silly name stuck. It seemed to them that this Catholic priest was trying to bring God into science. After all, if the universe has just always been there, you can sort of ignore God. But if it actually had a beginning...

Fr. Lemaître didn't argue theology. He just kept pointing to the evidence and making calculations. And one by one, the scientists—people like Einstein, who had first been skeptical of the idea—came around and had to admit that it was the only explanation that made sense. Fr. Lemaître—who became Msgr. Lemaître in 1960—lived long enough to see his theory go from some crazy semi-religious notion to the standard scientific explanation of the phenomena.

So we know that the universe did have a beginning. And according to the best calculations, that beginning was about 13,800,000,000 years ago.

I have a hard time imagining 13.8 billion years. But some scientists came up with a clever way to help us imagine it. Imagine if all that history were compressed into one year. How much of that would be human history?

The Cosmic Calendar

We start with the big bang at midnight on January 1.

It takes almost all winter before the galaxy we live in forms. The Milky Way is finally in place on March 16.

Now we can take a long vacation, because the solar system doesn't come together until it's almost fall—about September 2, with the oldest rocks on earth dating from about September 6.

Once the earth was formed, life got right to work. It looks as though the first life came about the beginning of fall—September 21. Maybe a little earlier: scientists aren't quite sure yet, and maybe they never will be. Anyway, this isn't the kind of life you want to be. This is just very simple life, like bacteria, and that's all you're going to get for the next month and a half.

But on the last day of September, some of those simple forms of life learn to do something very interesting. They start to photosynthesize. You learned about photosynthesis in elementary-school science class: it's what plants do to make their own food. They take in carbon dioxide and put out oxygen. And that's very important, because before there was no significant oxygen in the atmosphere. Now, with these simple cells photosynthesizing as hard as they can, it only takes a billion years—a little less than a month, October 29 in our calendar—to pump enough oxygen into the air to make a place where, for the first time, we could live without a breathing tank.

But we're not there yet. We don't even have animals. We don't even have life with more than one cell. That doesn't happen till December 5.

A couple of days later, a week into the last month of the year, we get the first animals.

Halfway through December, we get bugs. Now we're cookin'!

On Christmas Day, December 25, the first dinosaurs appear. (Don't get too attached to them.). A day later, the first little mammals appear and get stepped on by dinosaurs.

On December 27, some of those dinosaurs start looking a lot like birds.

On December 28, we get flowers for the first time.

On December 30, something awful happens, and all the dinosaurs except the birds die out.

Okay, we're running out of time here. It's the last day of the year, and we still haven't got to humans yet.

Halfway through the last day, and we still haven't got to humans.

Ten P.M. on the last day, and we still haven't got to humans.

Finally, it's 10:24 P.M. on December 31, and we begin to see creatures that look more or less human making simple stone tools.

It's not till 11:44 P.M. that these humans figure out how fire works.

Halfway through the last minute of the year—11:59:32 P.M.—we finally invent farming.

More than three-quarters of the way through that last minute, at 11:59:47, we start to write things down. Now we have history—for the last thirteen seconds of the year.

Five seconds before the end of the year, at 11:59:55 PM., Jesus Christ is born—*in the fullness of time!!!* (see Galatians 4:4-5)

We're living in the fullness of time. We have to cram all the history that's happened since then into five seconds—Roman Empire, Dark Ages, Byzantine Empire, Middle Ages, Crusades, Renaissance, printing, discovery of America, Guadalupe, industrial age, electric light, two world wars, computers, moon landing, Internet.

Isn't *that* something to try to wrap your head around?

Five seconds away from Year 1

We think of two thousand years as a long time. But you've been in a room with twenty people—a class, or a meeting, or a café that's not too busy. It's not a lot of people. And these days, with modern medical care, any one of us could live to be a hundred years old.

So the next time you're in a room with twenty people, think to yourself: I'm looking at two thousand years of history. You can visualize two thousand years of history that easily.

One day I met a fellow from Minneapolis who traded in coins. His name was Don. He loved to talk about old coins, and he made the topic sound very interesting. At least it was interesting to me—I was fascinated by what he told me. And I started thinking. "Don," I said, "is there any way I could get a coin from the time of Christ—you know, a Roman coin—or are those, like, only in museums and not for sale?"

He looked at me very seriously and said, "Well, Father, for you, *today only*... $9.95." Then he broke into a big smile. "I'll sell it to you for nine dollars and ninety-five cents."

"What do you mean?"

"They're as easy to get as water," he said. "There are coins from two thousand years ago all over the place. They're not a rare item."

And he was right, of course. I've looked up Roman coins since that conversation. Depending on the coin, $9.95 might have been too much to pay.

So why am I telling you all these things? I want to give you a sense of history, a sense of the moment we're living in. I want you to see that *Christ did not live all that long ago.*

We're actually pretty close to that moment in history where everything changed—the moment that divides everything into *before* and *after*. *Before* is a long time—364 days, 23 hours, 59 minutes, 55 seconds, according to our one-year calendar of all time since creation. *After* is five seconds at the end of the last day. We're still so close that people are always stumbling on Roman pennies dropped on the ground and never picked up.

And who was there to see everything change? Mary. She was right there at the crossroads of history.

Now, I have to tell you from the start that this book takes a Eurocentric look at history. We're not going into Asian history or African history or Polynesian history—it's pretty much a Western European Christian history. I'm doing that because it's the history most of my readers know about, and because it's the history *I* know about, which is at least as important. But I don't want you to think that, just because I talk mostly about European history, Mary doesn't have anything to do with the history of the rest of the world. No, she's there, everywhere, as much in Africa and Asia and Polynesia as in Europe.

The best place to start with history is at the beginning. No, not the big bang, but the beginning of human history. We're going back to the first book in the Bible.

A sneak preview of the Gospel

In fact we're going back to Genesis 3:15.

We know the story up to that point. God creates the world and then puts a man and a woman in it. He gives them a nice garden with everything they could possibly want to eat. And there's only *one rule*. And what do Adam and Eve go and do? Of course they break the one rule. They eat the fruit from the tree of the knowledge of good and evil.

The serpent made us do it, Eve says. "The serpent tricked me into it, so I ate it."

Well, that doesn't matter, does it? You had only one rule, and you broke it. You *knew* there were going to be consequences. Consequences are what naturally follow from sin.

But even before he gets to the consequences, God has a little piece of good news for Adam and Eve—and a great big piece of bad news for the Serpent.

Then the LORD God said to the serpent:

"Because you have done this, you shall be banned
    from all the animals
    and from all the wild creatures;
On your belly shall you crawl,
    and dirt shall you eat
    all the days of your life.
I will put enmity between you and the woman,
    and between your offspring and hers;
He will strike at your head,
    while you strike at his heel." [Genesis 3:14-15.]

This passage is known as the Protevangelium, which is Greek for "First Gospel." It's like a sneak preview of the Gospel. Adam and Eve learn the Lord will send into the world a Savior to redeem us from our sins, and he will actually crush the head of the devil who had tempted Adam and Eve and rebelled against God. And it will be the *woman*, Mary, who will be the mother of that child.

Now pay close attention here. You might have to read the next seven lines two or three times to get it.

The word that the New American Bible translates as "offspring" is actually the word for "seed" in Greek. The Bible never talks about the "seed" of a woman. Women have sons or daughters, but when the Bible talks about offspring as "seed" it's always the "seed" of a man.

Except here.

It seems to be saying that the woman will have offspring without a man at all. And there was only one woman in history who did that.

Mary is right there at the beginning of human history, at least in a prophetic and hopeful form. The *first* crossroads of history.

B.C. and A.D.

Now we're going to move ahead thousands of years. (Fundamentalists will tell you it was four thousand four years, but I think it might be a little longer than that.) We're heading for the date March 25.

What's March 25? March 25 is the day that Frodo puts the ring into the crack of doom.

I don't know if you're a Tolkien fan, but that really jumped off the page for me. Usually Tolkien is speaking mythological language, but that date has an obvious Christian reference. What happened on March 25 of the year 1 A.D.? The angel Gabriel appeared to Mary.

> And in the sixth month, the angel Gabriel was sent from God into a city of Galilee, called Nazareth, to a virgin espoused to a man whose name was Joseph, of the house of David; and the virgin's name was Mary. And the angel, having come in, said to her: "Hail, full of grace, the Lord is with thee:[1] blessed art thou among women." [Luke 1:26-28, Douay-Rheims version, language slightly modernized.]

It's not every day an angel shows up in your house. You can imagine that Mary was a little surprised.

> But she was greatly troubled at what was said and pondered what sort of greeting this might be.
>
> Then the angel said to her, "Do not be afraid, Mary, for you have found favor with God. Behold, you will conceive in your womb and bear a son, and you shall name him Jesus. He will be great and will be called Son of the Most High, and the Lord God will give him the throne of David his father, and he will rule over the house of Jacob forever, and of his kingdom there will be no end." [Luke 1:29-33.]

Well, that's pretty amazing news. Mary, though, wasn't quite sure what to make of it, and she asked the obvious question:

---

[1] "Ave gratia plena: Dominus tecum," in the Latin Vulgate.

But Mary said to the angel, "How can this be, since I have no relations with a man?"

And the angel said to her in reply, "The holy Spirit will come upon you, and the power of the Most High will overshadow you. Therefore the child to be born will be called holy, the Son of God." [Luke 1:34-35.]

In other words, the child is going to have a human mother, but no *human* father. He will be the offspring—the *seed*—of the *woman*.

This is why March 25 is known as the Feast of the Annunciation: because the angel came to announce the coming birth. And of course Jesus was conceived as soon as Mary said, "Behold, I am the handmaid of the Lord. May it be done to me according to your word." [Luke 1:38.]

There's the event that breaks history in two. All time before that is known as B.C.—*before Christ.* All time after that is known as A.D.—*anno Domini*—"in the Year of the Lord." Unless you've been influenced by anti-historical revisionist history that substitutes B.C.E. and C.E. for B.C. and A.D.

B.C.E. means "before the Common Era," and C.E. means the "Common Era."

But those designations beg the question. What's "common" about it?

Oh, we don't want to talk about that, because that's Christ.

But we simply can't get away from the historical fact of his life if we are honest. The birth of Christ divides everything into *before* and *after*.

Look at your calendar. I'm looking at mine now: it tells me the date is January 15, 2020 A.D. That's the date here in Chicago, it's the date in New York City, it's the date in Paris, it's the date in Rome, it's the date in Istanbul, it's the date in Lagos, it's the date in Beijing, You cannot escape this historical fact of the birth of Jesus Christ two thousand years ago. You cannot escape the fact that the coming of Christ divides history in two. Much as you want to redefine it, you cannot escape it.

(And that's true, by the way, even if historians made a bit of a mistake about the dating. Some people estimate that Christ was actually born in

4 B.C, or 3 or 5 B.C. Doesn't matter. The point is that the whole world's calendar is meant to count from the birth of Christ.)

And who was there at the very beginning?

Mary, who said yes.

Mary's yes changed history. The *second* crossroads in history.

So we go forward. Nine months later, it's Christmas Day.

How do we know Jesus Christ was born on December 25?

Well, a lot of people will say that he wasn't, and that Christians simply appropriated that date because it was a Roman holiday. And if Christians "appropriated that date," then maybe the birth and life of Christ was just a myth. But the life of Christ is not a man-made myth: we have extraordinary evidence for his existence, and sound evidence and reasoning for his birthdate on December 25.

Think about it. Who knew he was born on December 25? His mother knew it. Joseph knew it. The shepherds—well, they may not have known, because they may not have even known what the calendar was. They certainly knew the seasons, and they wouldn't have forgotten the day when they saw the sky filled with angels. The wise men from the East showed up some time later, but they were wise men, after all—probably into astrology, which meant they knew their dates backwards and forwards. I'm guessing they knew exactly when the King of the Jews was scheduled to be born, because God allowed it to be revealed to them through their stellar calculations.

So there are a good number of people who *probably* knew when the birth happened. But we know for sure that Mary and Joseph knew the day Jesus was born, because they were there. And I'm sure they told Jesus the day, just the way our parents told us. And the apostles would have learned that from Mary, or Jesus, or both.

The first time December 25 shows up in any written records is 350 A.D. Now, of course, that's just counting the written records we still have. Historians estimate that 90% of all writing from classical antiquity has disappeared. And that's just the important stuff—things that would qualify as literature. When you get to things like public records and private correspondence, we're lucky to have anything at all. So it's very possible that written records were there, but we've lost three hundred years' worth of them. It's also possible that this important information was passed on by word of mouth by the early Christians.[2]

It's very fitting that Jesus was born on the day the ancient Romans regarded as the winter solstice, although by 350 the calendar was off by four days. At the winter solstice, the days start getting longer, and more light comes into the world. And Jesus is the Light of the world.

So December 25 is the first very important day in Jesus' life. And what's the next great important day in Jesus' life that changed the world completely?

His death.

And who was there?

Mary, with John, at the foot of the cross.

There she is, at the hardest, the saddest, the most devastating moment of her life—and our redemption is accomplished.

Once again, Mary stands at the crossroads of history.

Pentecost and beyond

After the crucifixion, the next time we see Mary in the Bible is sitting in the upper room with the apostles.

> When they entered the city they went to the upper room where they were staying, Peter and John and James and Andrew, Philip and Thomas, Bartholomew and Matthew, James son of Alphaeus, Simon the Zealot, and Judas son of James. All these devoted themselves with one accord to prayer, together with some women, and Mary the mother of Jesus, and his brothers. [Acts 1:13-14.]

---

[2] For a scholarly exposition on the actual birthday of Jesus Christ, cf. *Towards the Origins of Christmas,* by Susan K. Roll (Kok Pharos Publishing House, 1995).

This was the core group of Jesus' followers after he ascended into heaven: the apostles, "some women," the brothers of Jesus (who were actually his cousins, but the Greek uses the word "brothers" in a broader sense than we do), and Mary. They spent their time in the same upper room where Jesus had eaten the Last Supper with his disciples. And they spend their time praying.

I've always wondered: do you suppose the Rosary was born during that original novena, with the apostles and the Mother of God praying in the Upper Room, remembering how the angel had announced the coming of the Messiah?

I don't know the answer. But I do know that they were all there on the day of Pentecost.

> When the time for Pentecost was fulfilled, they were all in one place together. And suddenly there came from the sky a noise like a strong driving wind, and it filled the entire house in which they were. Then there appeared to them tongues as of fire, which parted and came to rest on each one of them. And they were all filled with the holy Spirit and began to speak in different tongues, as the Spirit enabled them to proclaim. [Acts 2:1-4.]

This is the birthday of the Church: the beginning of the spread of Christianity to the world. Three thousand people were baptized on that one day. And once again Mary was there.

Now, the Church makes a list of seven "gifts of the Holy Spirit"— qualities that the coming of the Spirit gives to us:

1. Wisdom
2. Understanding
3. Counsel
4. Fortitude
5. Knowledge
6. Piety

7. Fear of the Lord.

And you can't imagine anyone who makes those qualities more obvious than Mary. By the special grace that was given to her even before she was born, she had them all from the very beginning.

First, *wisdom*—something she had to have quite a lot of, because her life was full of choices, and they weren't easy choices. Wisdom aligns your mind with your heart. It was a very wise woman who said, "Behold, I am the handmaid of the Lord. May it be done to me according to your word."

Understanding is what we need to recognize what God's purpose is. It's more of an intellectual thing than wisdom is. Again, think of Mary's response to the Annunciation. Think of her at Cana (see John 2), when she knew exactly what to do when the wedding party ran out of wine. She knew that because she had the gift of understanding her Son's purpose, even when he seemed to be reluctant.

Counsel is a little different from wisdom and understanding. It's the ability to make the right decision right now—to know what God wants from us when we have to make a choice. Both at the Annunciation and at Cana, Mary showed that ability.

Fortitude is being able to stick to God's purpose even when it's really, really hard. I can't imagine anything harder than watching your own Son be tortured to death. Yet Mary was there. She didn't go off somewhere else because she couldn't stand to watch—which, frankly, is what you or I probably would have done. She stayed there at the foot of the cross the whole time. And the source of that Fortitude was her years of prayer and deep contemplation pondering the Word of God from the Old Testament, and meditating on the prophecies, especially found in the Book of Isaiah, and particularly that section about the "suffering servant"—a passage that would give her strength later at the foot of the cross, because all she had read was coming true right in front of her very own eyes.

Knowledge is the gift we need to be able to exercise the gift of counsel. Mary had to *know* that Jesus was able to help out with the wine problem, and she had to know that it was time for him to begin to reveal himself to the world. Then the gift of counsel allowed her to make the right decision based on that knowledge.

Piety is the ability to give God what we owe to him: our love and reverence for him as our Father, and our love and respect for other people as his children. We see that in Mary both in the way she does what God wills and keeps up an active prayer life and in the way she responds to the needs of other people around her, as she did at Cana. Piety is affection for God that springs from the human heart.

Finally, *fear of the Lord* is a sense of the real greatness of God. It's fear not in the sense of fearing some faceless danger, but in the same way that we might be afraid of disappointing our parents. When we have the right kind of fear of the Lord, we avoid doing anything that might damage our relationship with God. We literally never see Mary doing anything in Scripture that doesn't show this healthy and joyful fear of the Lord. In everything she does, God's will comes first.

Mary had all these gifts from the beginning, because she was full of grace. But she was there when the Holy Spirit came down on all the followers of Jesus who were gathered there in that upper room. The gifts of the Spirit were poured out on everybody, just as Jesus had promised they would be.

And what happened next was practically an explosion. Everything changed for the better in an instant.

Three thousand people baptized on one day! They had to set up an assembly line for baptisms.

Before Pentecost, the infant Church had been stagnant. They just sat in the room and waited, praying. They were afraid to go out, because after all, what had happened to Jesus might happen to them next. There were powerful people out there who were determined to make sure that this Jesus movement went nowhere.

Not that it's a bad thing to spend your time in prayer. Quite the reverse. You spend your time in prayer *because* you want Pentecost to happen. You pray for the gifts of the Spirit so that you'll have the power to do what God wants of you.

And that was what the followers of Jesus did. They prayed, and they got what they prayed for.

Now they're not hiding anymore. Now they're out there proclaiming the Gospel to anyone who will listen.

And they find three thousand listeners.

Ever since then, Mary has been there whenever the Church is filled with missionary zeal. She drives us forward to tell the world the Good News about her Son. Think of the organizations that are growing most today: the Missionaries of Charity, Opus Dei. What do they have in common? They have an intense devotion to Mary.

And Mary doesn't forget that.

She's with us in our missionary efforts now, just as much as she was with the apostles at that first Pentecost. There's a reason we call her the Mother of the Church.

And there's a story about how she was with St. James in his missionary efforts, just when he was ready to give up.

Our Lady of the Pillar

According to an ancient tradition, the apostles divided the world up among them. Each went to a different part of the world, as they knew it, to spread the Good News. And the two who went farthest were Thomas and James.

Thomas went to India, according to a very ancient tradition. There have been Christians in India since before there were Christians in most of Western Europe, and even today they consider themselves Thomas Christians—people whose Indian church was founded by Thomas the Apostle.

James went in exactly the opposite direction. He ended up in Spain, as far west as you could get (unless you discovered America, which James didn't do). And there he had a rough time of it.

James was fed up with the Spaniards. And I have a lot of Spanish friends—I can understand it. They are strong people, and not easily per-suaded.

So James was really ready to pack it in and call the whole mission a failure.

But when he sat down to pray by the river near what is now Zaragoza, Mary appeared to him.

This was very strange, because Mary was still alive and on earth at the time, and she was living in Jerusalem. But James saw her right there in Spain, standing on a pillar—a classical Roman column in the square—with angels swirling around her.

That got James' attention.

He had been ready to give up, but Mary granted him this special visit to encourage him to keep going. And she had a prophecy of the future for him. Look, she said, if these people in Spain convert, they'll take the faith all over the world. She told him to build a church there, and the people would come to that spot and pray.

So James did keep going. According to tradition, he built the first church in Spain near that very spot where Mary had appeared to him—the first apparition of Mary in Christian history. And we know that the spot has been associated with Mary since very early times. Ancient Christian tombs nearby have frescoes of the Assumption of the Blessed Virgin. Obviously Zaragoza was a center of devotion to Mary even back in the days of the Roman Empire.

As for Our Lady's prophecy about the Spanish—well, we'll be coming back to Spain more than once to see how that worked out.

3. Mother of God, Mother of the Church

Mary doesn't appear in Scripture after Pentecost—except for the glorious vision in the middle of the book of Revelation.

> A great sign appeared in the sky, a woman clothed with the sun, with the moon under her feet, and on her head a crown of twelve stars. She was with child and wailed aloud in pain as she labored to give birth.
>
> Then another sign appeared in the sky; it was a huge red dragon, with seven heads and ten horns, and on its heads were seven diadems. Its tail swept away a third of the stars in the sky and hurled them down to the earth. Then the dragon stood before the woman about to give birth, to devour her child when she gave birth. She gave birth to a son, a male child, destined to rule all the nations with an iron rod. Her child was caught up to God and his throne. The woman herself fled into the desert where she had a place prepared by God, that there she might be taken care of for twelve hundred and sixty days. [Revelation 12:1-6.]

Revelation, or the Apocalypse, is just about the hardest book to interpret in all of Scripture. It's filled with dense layers of images and symbols, and Scripture scholars can spend whole careers trying to peel them apart.

But if you're Mexican or Latin American, or if you have neighbors who are Mexican or Latin American, you recognize that image right away: "a woman clothed with the sun, with the moon under her feet." It's Our Lady of Guadalupe.

In context, the vision certainly makes us think of Mary. But the woman here has also been interpreted several other ways. She is the old Israel, giving birth to the new Israel, the Church. Or she is the Church,

giving birth to us, her sons and daughters. In the layers and layers of sym-
bolism, these interpretations can all be true at once. What we end up
with is a picture of Mary as the Mother of the Church.

And that's the picture the Bible leaves us. But tradition has more to
say.

Assumed into heaven

What Christian tradition tells us about Mary is that, just as Jesus had
intended, she lived out the rest of her life with John the Apostle. When
the end of her life came, she was taken up into heaven to be with her Son
forever. That's what Christians have believed from the very earliest times,
although some Protestants don't accept it anymore. We call this being
taken into heaven the *Assumption* of the Virgin Mary, and it's a big feast
in the Church calendar on August 15.

Since Christians have believed in the Assumption for centuries, it's
surprising that the doctrine wasn't officially in place until the middle of
the twentieth century. In 1950, Pope Pius XII finally defined the Assumption as a dogma of the Catholic Church. But he pointed out that
he was only defining what had already been the belief and practice of the
Church since very early times.

As Pope Pius explained in *Munificentissimus Deus,* the document that
formally defined the dogma, the Assumption of Mary is rooted in what
we know about the intimate relationship between Christ and his
Mother. All mortals die, even the good ones, and their bodies decay. But,
just as grace preserved Mary from the original sin that all other human
beings inherit, it also preserved her from the decay that everyone else goes
through.

> Now God has willed that the Blessed Virgin Mary should be
> exempted from this general rule. She, by an entirely unique
> privilege, completely overcame sin by her Immaculate Concep-
> tion, and as a result she was not subject to the law of remaining

in the corruption of the grave, and she did not have to wait until the end of time for the redemption of her body....

All these proofs and considerations of the holy Fathers and the theologians are based upon the Sacred Writings as their ultimate foundation. These set the loving Mother of God as it were before our very eyes as most intimately joined to her divine Son and as always sharing his lot. Consequently it seems impossible to think of her, the one who conceived Christ, brought him forth, nursed him with her milk, held him in her arms, and clasped him to her breast, as being apart from him in body, even though not in soul, after this earthly life. Since our Redeemer is the Son of Mary, he could not do otherwise, as the perfect observer of God's law, than to honor, not only his eternal Father, but also his most beloved Mother. And, since it was within his power to grant her this great honor, to preserve her from the corruption of the tomb, we must believe that he really acted in this way.[3]

And what's the basis for this in Scripture? (When you live surrounded by non-Catholic Christians, that question always occurs to you.) The biggest one is that vision in Revelation—the woman clothed with the sun. John looked into heaven and saw Mary there.

In the Eastern churches, the belief is that Mary "fell asleep"—that means suffered a natural death—but was resurrected and taken into heaven. That falling asleep is called the "Dormition" of the Blessed Virgin, and you often see Orthodox churches dedicated to the Dormition. In the Roman Catholic Church, some people believe she didn't die and was taken straight up to heaven, and others believe she did die first. That part of the doctrine isn't defined, and like a lot of other things in Catholicism, you're free to believe what makes sense to you and still be a good Catholic.

---

[3] Pope Pius XII, *Munificentissimus Deus*, 5, 38.

There's also some disagreement about where it happened. Mary was living with John, and some say they were at Ephesus at the time. There's also a tradition that they were back in Jerusalem. Again, you're free to research it yourself and believe what makes sense.

The important thing to know is that Jesus' Mother is with him all the time. That's only fitting. The Mother of God should be with her Son. With Jesus, our brother. There she can be Mother to all of us—Mother of the Church. Because God chose her as his own Mother, she's honored as Queen of Heaven.

And now I'm going to jump forward about four centuries to the first time when somebody tried to push Mary off her throne.

Mother of God or Mother of the Christ?

It's the year 428, and Constantinople needs a new archbishop.

Constantinople has long since become the most important city in the Roman Empire. It's the capital of the eastern half, and the western half isn't doing very well. Old Rome is busy being invaded by barbarians, but the shining city of Constantinople is rich and prosperous.

And Rome is a Christian empire now. Christianity is the official religion, which means that the emperor is involved in picking the archbishop for the capital city of the eastern half of the empire.

So who should get the job? Next to the pope, this is the most important position in the Church, so it's got to be someone who's up to the task.

Fortunately there's a man who seems to have all the right qualifications. He's a priest in Antioch—another big important city in the eastern empire—who's been making a name for himself as a preacher. They say he's got quite a brain on him, too. And he was the disciple of one of the most famous Christian teachers in the East. Sold! He sounds like just the archbishop Constantinople needs.

And so Nestorius comes to Constantinople. And pretty soon there are riots in the streets.

The problem was one Greek word. But it was one Greek word that said everything the people of Constantinople believed about Mary.

The word was *Theotokos*. We translate it as "Mother of God." That's one of the titles Christians have always used for Mary.

And Nestorius told people to stop using it.

You could call Mary "Mother of the Christ"—*Christotokos* in Greek. That was all right, he said. But a human woman couldn't be mother of God. She was only the mother of the human part of Christ.

Heads exploded all over Constantinople. "Mother of God" is *exactly* what Mary is, people said. You can't rip Christ's human nature apart from his divine nature. The two natures are inseparable. Christ is one person, and Mary gave birth to the whole package, God and man.

If Mary isn't Mother of God, then *Christ isn't God*.

It didn't help that Nestorius was a fussy intellectual snob. If you disagreed with him, he treated you as if you were just too stupid to understand. That didn't make him more popular in Constantinople, which was full of people who were just as smart as Nestorius and liked to have it acknowledged.

News traveled faster than you'd think in those days. Ships went everywhere in the East, and soon everyone had heard of Nestorius and the big fight in Constantinople. The pope in Rome took time off from cleaning up after barbarians to condemn these new ideas. Nestorius was not impressed by that. Who did the bishop of Rome think he was? Constantinople was a bigger and more important city, so Nestorius must be a bigger and more important bishop.

But things didn't calm down. The fights only got worse. And Nestorius asked the emperor to do the one thing he was sure would settle the whole thing. If the emperor would call all the bishops together in a council of the whole Church, surely they would see everything Nestorius' way. Especially if the council could be held in Constantinople, where things might...happen...to bishops who opposed Nestorius.

Fair enough, said the emperor. He called a council in 431. But the council would be at Ephesus, away from all the fuss.

The Council of Ephesus

And that was bad news for Nestorius, because Ephesus was the place that claimed the home of Our Lady in her later years. It was a big pilgrimage site. People in Ephesus were *completely* devoted to Our Lady. And furthermore, they were willing to do something about it. In those days, theology was popular entertainment. A technical argument could turn into mob violence very quickly.

So Nestorius made sure he was protected. He went there with a squadron of soldiers to make sure things went smoothly.

The president of the council was Cyril of Alexandria (we know him as St. Cyril now), one of the most powerful thinkers of the Church at that time, or any time. He had the pope's authorization to deal with the Nestorius problem on his behalf, and he had already been Nestorius' most vocal and most persuasive opponent.

Nestorius was furious to see that his old enemy Cyril was in charge. The emperor, when he called the council, had left very explicit instructions that it was to start on time no matter what, but Nestorius wanted to wait till some of his friends from Syria could get there. He was furious again when Cyril insisted on following the emperor's instructions and opened the council on time. In fact, Nestorius spent most of the council being furious. He was especially furious when the council condemned his doctrine, and then him for refusing to back down.

It turned into an even bigger mess when a small group of Nestorius' supporters declared themselves the real Council of Ephesus. Nestorius' soldiers arrested all the other bishops and refused to let them leave, and even stopped the food supplies. People started to get sick. Bishops were dying almost every day. Meanwhile, there were huge anti-Nestorius demonstrations in Constantinople, just in case the emperor had any doubts about where his people stood on the issue.

It took months to sort out, but eventually the emperor decreed that Cyril's council had been the real Council of Ephesus. Mary was Mother of God: that was official doctrine of the Catholic Church. Nestorius was wrong.

There were huge celebrations back in the capital of Constantinople. The system worked! Granted, it took a few riots and things, but the system worked. What Christians had always known to be true was accepted as official doctrine by the universal Church.

But there were some Eastern Christians who never accepted that decree. It had been a big fight, after all, and there were a lot of hard feelings. The ones who had supported Nestorius went home muttering to themselves, and they never reconciled with the Catholic Church after that. They led their congregations into schism, insisting that Mary was *not* Mother of God.

And where were most of those schismatic congregations?

Syria, Iraq, Afghanistan—places like that.

What happened to Syria, Iraq, and Afghanistan 200 years later?

Those were the parts of the Christian world that became Muslim.

The error that changes history

The Muslim conquest was amazingly swift. Mohammed died in 632. Thirty years later, what are today Syria, Iraq, Iran, and a big chunk of Afghanistan were already ruled by Muslims. And they have been Muslim countries ever since.

Why so fast?

Well, part of it was the endless cycle of wars between East and West. The Roman Empire (or what was left of it, which we call the Byzantine Empire today) and the Persian Empire had been fighting most of the time for hundreds of years. They were both pretty well worn out when the Arab armies started coming after them.

But that doesn't seem like enough of an explanation. I think you have to consider how close these areas were to being Muslim already.

To understand that, we have to understand something about what Muslims believe. We have to look into that third great world religion that comes from the faith of Abraham.

Most of the people I know in America who aren't Muslim themselves have only a vague idea of what Muslims believe. They know that Muslims believe in one God, and they know they aren't Christians. But what they don't know is how important Jesus and Mary are in Muslim belief.

Muslims will tell you Jesus was a great guy, and Mary was a virgin. But Jesus is a man, not God, and Mary is the mother of Jesus, not the mother of God. This is the fundamental difference between Christians and Muslims.

Both Jesus and Mary are big deals in the Koran. In fact, if you read the Koran, you start to realize that Islam is basically a detour from Christianity. What I mean is that it's the Christian faith, but with one change that makes everything different.

To understand Islam, then, I think we have to go back to where it began.

Mohammed was a merchant in Mecca in Arabia, which was kind of on the fringes of civilization, as far as people in the Roman Empire were concerned. Trade routes went through Arabia, though, so you got all kinds of people there. Some were Christians, some were Jews, and a lot were still pagans who practiced traditional desert religions.

It seems that Mohammed was fairly well off: he married a wealthy widow fifteen years older than himself. As a young man he had spent time buying and selling in the Christian lands of the Roman Empire, so he was very familiar with Christian civilization. Furthermore, there were Christians in his wife's family, including one cousin—a Jewish convert to Christianity—who had translated some of the Bible into Arabic. So even though Mohammed couldn't read and write, he knew a lot about the world, and something about Christian and Jewish belief. With this wife (he had several others, but only after she died) Mohammed had several children. But only one lived to adulthood, at least according to one strand of Islamic tradition: his beloved daughter Fatima. Fatima is a big deal in the Islamic world. Throughout Islamic history, Fatima has been just about the most popular name for girls. And that little fact will actually come into our story in a few centuries, so keep it in the back of your mind.

When he was forty years old, Mohammed started to have visions. The angel Gabriel came to him and revealed to him that he was the last and greatest of the prophets.

After that, Mohammed had revelations every so often, and those revelations make up the Koran.

The basic theme of Islam is that the God of Abraham is the only true God, just as Jews and Christians believe. But the true faith of Abraham got corrupted along the way. Muslims believe that both Jews and Christians have added things that God never intended to be there.

So in the Koran Jesus is the Messiah, and he was miraculously born of the Virgin Mary. But he is still only a human being,

A lot of text is devoted to Mary in the Koran. It tells the traditional story of her birth—which isn't found in the New Testament, but which has been told in Christian literature since very early times. The Annunciation is there, too. Mary miraculously gives birth to Jesus, because God wills it to be so.

But Jesus is not God's son. "It is not fitting for God to have a son. Glory be to him! When he decrees a thing, he only says to it, 'Be,' and it is."[4]

Jews and Christians are People of the Book: they follow the Scriptures, which do contain revelations from God, though corrupted ones. So they're better off than pagans, in the Muslim way of thinking. Where Christians go seriously wrong is when they say that there are three Gods, which seems to be how Mohammed interprets the Trinity. "People of the Book! Do not overstep the bounds in your religion, and speak only truth of God. The Messiah, Jesus, son of Mary, is only an apostle of God, and his Word which he conveyed to Mary, and a Spirit proceeding from himself. Believe therefore in God and his apostles, and do not say 'Three.' Forbear! It will be better for you. God is only one God! Far be it from his glory that he should have a son!"[5]

---

[4] Koran, Sura 19, translated by J. M. Rodwell, with the language modernized.

[5] Koran, Sura 4, translated by J. M. Rodwell, with the language modernized.

These are just Nestorius' ideas taken to their logical conclusion. The people in Constantinople were right. If Mary is not Mother of God, then Jesus is not God. That's where you get if you start denying that Mary is Mother of God.

This is the error that changes history. This is what gives us our world today.

Still, it is a fact that Muslims honor Mary above all other women—even above Fatima, the daughter of Mohammed, whom they view as the second-most-fortunate woman in the world after Mary. In fact, Muslims pay more attention to Mary than a lot of Protestant Christians do. And that's another thing we have to keep in mind if we want to understand the Muslim world and build bridges instead of picking fights. Mary is a bridge.

Anyway, as I said, the way the Muslims saw Christ and Mary was just one step further down the path of Nestorianism. So many of the Eastern Christians had no trouble accepting the new faith—especially when the alternative was the sword. They were hemmed in on both sides: the Byzantine Empire had been purging heretics, so they had that to worry about if the Byzantines won. The Muslims may well have represented an easier choice.

I should mention, though, that there is kind of a small happy ending to the story of these Nestorian Christians, that minority group who split off from the Church after the Council of Ephesus. Although the countries around them became Muslim, some of those Christians kept the faith century after century. They dwindled into small minorities, but they were still there.

And just in my own lifetime, the centuries of animosity and disagreement between those Eastern Christians and the Catholic Church were finally wiped away. In 1994, Patriarch Dinkha IV of the Assyrian Church of the East and Pope John Paul II agreed to a "Common Christological Declaration"—a document that basically says, after all these centuries, we believe the same things about Christ and his Mother. The Catholic Church agrees that it is perfectly correct to call Mary the Mother of

Christ our God and Savior, as the Assyrian Church does, and the Assyrian Church agrees that it is perfectly correct to call Mary the Mother of God.

There are still a few differences between the two churches, but they are small enough that members of one church can receive the Eucharist from the other.

Unfortunately, the Eastern churches are dwindling even more. Christians are constant targets for violence in the unending turmoil in the Middle East. But we can thank God that the Nestorian schism is—mostly—over at last.

And I like to think Mary's prayers had a lot to do with that.

Meanwhile, with the East under their control, the conquering Muslim armies spilled all the way across North Africa. The land of Tertullian, St. Augustine, St. Cyprian, all those great names in Christian thought—it was all under Muslim domination now.

What was next?

The obvious target was Europe.

4. The Confrontation in Spain

It's the year 711—less than eighty years after the death of Mohammed. The Caliphate, the empire of Islam, stretches from India in the east all the way to Morocco in the west.

And here they come into Spain.

Take a look at a map of Europe. Look down in the lower left corner at the entrance to the Mediterranean Sea. That's the Strait of Gibraltar, and it's less than nine miles wide. That's all that separates Europe from North Africa. You can sit in Africa and see Europe across the water. And if you're in a conquering mood, you might think to yourself, a few soldiers, a few boats...

Crossing into Europe

The Caliphate at the time was one of the largest empires the world had ever known. It was already more than double the size the Roman Empire had been at its greatest extent, and it was still gobbling up territory. In fact, it was already a lot bigger than the entire continent of Europe—and the civilized part of Europe in those days was probably only half that area.

By any measurement, the Caliphate was huge. It was the most powerful force on earth.

It was also prosperous. And Europe was in pretty rough shape, especially in the West. It was the period we call the Dark Ages today—a time when life for most people was nasty, brutish, and short, in the famous words of Thomas Hobbes.

What made the Dark Ages dark?

Throughout the 400s, the Roman Empire in the West had been falling apart. (The eastern half, which we call the Byzantine Empire, did much better, and in fact it lasted for another thousand years, until 1453.) Barbarian conquerors chipped off provinces until there was nothing left. "Barbarian" was a word the Romans used for anyone who didn't speak Latin or Greek, and it would be unfair to the Goths, Franks, Burgundians, and other conquerors to suggest that they were stupid or inferior. But the net effect of all this constant destruction was that all the equipment of civilization broke down.

Big, prosperous cities were reduced to grubby little villages huddling in the ruins of their magnificent Roman buildings. Civilized things like reading and writing, common under the Roman Empire, became very rare. What really makes the Dark Ages dark is that we have so few records from that time. We know the basic outlines of the history. But the Roman Empire produced carloads of written records, and even with all the centuries of wars and disasters between us and them, we still have a lot of them. But the Dark Ages are almost a big hole in the history of Western Europe. In fact there's only one source for the Muslim invasion of Spain, which was one of the most important events in the whole period.

Spain (which included what is now Portugal) was a Christian kingdom ruled by Visigoths, the western division of the Gothic nation that had swept into the Roman Empire in the 400s. And in the year 711, Spain was in an even bigger mess than usual. There seems to have been some sort of civil war going on, with two different kings claiming the throne. One story (told centuries later) has it that one of the kings had an enemy who asked the Muslim rulers for help. Other sources suggest that the Muslim attackers only meant to make a few raids and earn some plunder, but found themselves unexpectedly winning battle after battle as the Christian armies abandoned their positions. The Christians were already worn out from fighting each other. There's a lesson in there, don't you think?

However the conquest started, it kept going. The Muslim army rolled up through Spain, winning battle after battle, hardly stopping for breath. They had gone almost all the way across from south to north, practically within shouting distance of the Bay of Biscay, the corner of the Atlantic Ocean that forms the northern edge of Spain.

And suddenly they stopped.

There, up in the mountains, was where Our Lady made her stand.

Turning back the tide

Stop and think for a moment how much was riding on the outcome of this confrontation. What would have happened if the armies of the Caliphate hadn't been stopped? Would Christians have been a persecuted minority in Europe, the way they are in Iraq or Syria? Would we have ever seen the glorious Gothic cathedrals of the Middle Ages? Would we have had the Renaissance, with Raphael and Da Vinci and Michelangelo? Would Europeans have found America?

I think the whole world would be different if the Caliphate hadn't been stopped. I think this is one of those inflection points in history, where everything is riding on what happens in one little corner of the earth.

But what *could* stop the seasoned conquering armies of the Caliphate? The kingdoms of Europe had no organization, and they were at least as likely to be fighting each other as to be banding together to fight an invader.

The few remnants of the Christian armies had taken refuge in the mountains at the northern edge of Spain. I suspect most Americans don't have any idea how far out of the way that is. Up in the eastern part of these mountains there are still, right now, a lot of people who speak Basque.

Basque is the most mysterious language in Europe. In fact it's one of the most mysterious languages in the world. Most languages are part of large families. You can tell that English, for example, is related to German, Dutch, Swedish, Icelandic, and all the other Germanic languages, and those are part of the larger Indo-European family that includes French and Russian and Hindi and more than four hundred others. But Basque isn't related to anything else on earth. The best theory about its origin is that it's a leftover from the languages people in Europe spoke before the prehistoric Indo-European invasions. This is the only part of Western Europe where anyone still speaks a language that ancient.

This mountain country is so isolated that the languages that took over *every other habitable part of the continent* could never quite take over here.

That's how desperate the Christian armies were. They fled to the most inaccessible spot in Europe.

And even there the Muslim armies were determined to root them out, as soon as they had a spare moment.

Other desperate people joined them to escape the Muslim rule that had been imposed on the rest of Spain (which, don't forget, included Portugal). The Christian refugees were hemmed into a strip of territory a few miles broad, with the armies of the Caliphate to the south and the ocean to the north.

For seven years they clung to a precarious existence in those mountains, just barely scraping enough out of the land to live on. And then things got a whole lot worse.

Covadonga

Just about ten miles from the shore of the Bay of Biscay, high in the mountains, there is a cave. It's a beautiful place. A rocky cliff interrupts the forest in the steep hills. A stream of clear water plunges off the cliff and pours roaring into a deep turquoise pool far below. Ferns and vines cling to the rocks. And in the middle of the cliff is a hole in the rock—the Holy Cave of Covadonga.

It's not the only cave in the area. The mountains are full of caves. But this one has a long history as a holy place. And that was the cave where a Christian leader named Pelagius came to pray in the year 722 (or whenever it was, because different historians give slightly different dates, and it's hard to pin a date down in the Dark Ages).

Pelagius—or Pelayo in modern Spanish—had been chosen as leader by the fractured remnants of the Christian armies. But it must have seemed to him as if he had been chosen just to die quickly and get it over with.

For a while he was able to hold off the small forces sent out to fight him, because the Caliphate was concentrating on other things and wasn't too worried about a few Christian guerrillas in the mountains. Pelagius and his band were a minor nuisance.

But now that they had pacified the rest of Spain, the armies of the Caliph were coming to the mountains. The commander was the seasoned general Al Qama, who had plans to clear out the holdouts. The Muslim conquerors weren't messing around, either. They didn't intend to spend a lot of time on this job. They were bringing an army big enough to make sure there could be no doubt about the outcome. They would get it over with quickly, and all of Spain would be theirs. Then they could concentrate on the rest of Europe.

You and I might say that Pelagius didn't have a prayer. But Pelagius preferred to think that he *did* have a prayer. There was a holy image of the Blessed Virgin in the cave, tended by hermits, and Pelagius knelt before the image to beg for Our Lady's help. He knew the odds were overwhelming. But he also knew there was powerful help against overwhelming odds.

And the army of the Caliphate kept marching.

Soon they were in the mountains, and Pelagius was waiting for them, very near that Holy Cave of Covadonga where he had prayed in front of Our Lady's image.

His soldiers must have thought they were doomed. The sound of clanking armor and thousands and thousands of marching feet filled the valleys and echoed off the mountains. The Muslims had every weapon the ingenuity of the East could provide them with. The Christians had rocks and logs.

Closer and closer the immense army came, until they were within a bowshot of the little Christian force.

Then suddenly the arrows started to fly. Al Qama's army let loose a barrage of arrows that darkened the sky. The Christians held up their shields to ward off as many as they could.

But something odd was happening. It seemed as though none of the arrows were hitting their targets. They were bouncing off the rocks. And —was it possible? Yes! The arrows were flying back at the archers who shot them!

Encouraged by what had to be a miracle of Our Lady, the Christians let their rocks and logs roll down on the Islamic horde.

And then came the storm. A terrific tempest uprooted trees and terrified Al Qama's men.

And then came the flood.

And then came the landslide.

Our Lady had really pulled out all the stops here. The Muslim army ran off in terror—or at least the ones who hadn't already been drowned in the flash flood or buried in the landslide. Pelagius and his men pursued them for miles. Informal Christian militias gathered from the villages all around and harried Al Qama's men as they ran.

Al Qama himself didn't survive to report his defeat—which was probably just as well for him. Things didn't go well for defeated generals in the Caliphate.

This was the first real Christian victory in Spain since the Muslims had invaded. And the Christians had no doubt who was responsible. Sure, they were grateful to Pelagius for his leadership. In fact, he became the first king of the Asturias—the tiny strip in the north that was all that was left of Christian Spain.

But Pelagius himself would have told them: it was Our Lady's victory.

Today there's a shrine in the Holy Cave, and a beautiful basilica nearby for the thousands of pilgrims who flock to Covadonga. They flock there because this is the birthplace of modern Spain. This was where the Reconquista began—the reconquest of Spain from the Muslim invaders.

It was a long process. In fact, it took until 1492.

You may remember that as an important year for another reason, but we'll talk about that later.

I was reading this story in a history by Warren H. Carroll. You may have heard of him. He founded Christendom College, a well-known

Catholic liberal-arts school in the Shenandoah Valley of Virginia. His *History of Christendom* is one of the best Catholic histories I've ever read. And when I came to the part about the Reconquista, one thing jumped off the page at me. He pointed out that the Reconquista was the longest war in world history.

Think about it. It started with the invasion of Spain in 711, and it wasn't over till 1492. That's 781 years, if you do a little math.

It would have been a lot shorter, though, if Pelagius hadn't had faith in Mary. When he prayed to Our Lady, he found the strength and the courage to push back against the Muslim invader, and that was what turned the tide. Maybe that was what saved all of Western Europe for Christianity.

Robert Southey was the Poet Laureate of Great Britain two hundred years ago, but he took so much interest in Spanish history that he was made a member of the Royal Spanish Academy and the Royal Spanish Academy of History. He wrote an epic poem about the Muslim conquest of Spain called *Roderick, the Last of the Goths*. And in his mind, Covadonga was the most significant spot in the whole country. Spain is drenched in history, but Southey said that no other place could compare.

> No holier spot than Covadonga Spain
> Boasts in her wide extent, though all her realms
> Be with the noblest blood of martyrdom
> In elder or in later days enriched,
> And glorified with tales of heavenly aid
> By many a miracle made manifest;
> Nor in the heroic annals of her fame
> Doth she show forth a scene of more renown.[6]

But what happened to all those Christians in Spain who didn't make it north to Asturias?

---

[6] Robert Southey, *Roderick, the Last of the Goths*, XVI.

They were still there. They lived for centuries under Muslim rulers, but they were still Christian. Many of them prospered—within the confines of what the Muslim government would allow. In fact, the combination of prosperous trade and an educated Christian population made Muslim Spain a haven for arts and culture unique in the world. Christian scholars took the remnants of classical Greek and Roman culture that were still preserved in the Caliphate and translated them into Latin, the language of culture in Western Europe.

And that would have an enormous influence on European culture later on, so Spain is still a place to watch.

But the Christians in Muslim Spain knew they had to be careful. Some of the Muslim rulers were tolerant. Some of them were cynical and indifferent. And some of them were brutally oppressive.

So if you were a Christian—as the majority were—you did your best to live a normal life. But if you had anything the Muslims might want to destroy, you put it away in a safe place.

One thing you could count on was that the Muslims were fierce iconoclasts. They considered any statue of a saint, any image of Mary or Christ, to be a kind of idolatry. "People of the book" could keep to their own religion, if they paid the special tax that non-Muslims had to pay, and if they didn't do anything that might offend the eyes or ears of a Muslim. You couldn't have religious processions in honor of saints' days, because a Muslim who saw the procession would be scandalized. You couldn't ring church bells, because Muslims could hear them. And if you had any images in your church, just the fact that they existed might be so offensive to some Muslim soldier that he would come looking for them to smash them to pieces.

Especially in the early excitement of the conquest, no one knows how many venerated images were smashed by the invaders.

And no one knows how many holy images in Spain were hidden away in secret places as the Muslim armies washed across the peninsula. But some of the most famous images in Spain have a time of hiding as part of their story.

Montserrat

Montserrat is a mountain that makes you think twice about going anywhere near it. In fact, "Montserrat" means "Sawtooth Mountain," and that's a perfect description. It's a row of jagged peaks like the teeth of a saw, sticking up more than four thousand feet at the highest point. If you wanted to hide something, up among those rocky points and cliffs would be a perfect place.

Way up in those rocks, stuck between the teeth like a piece of spinach, is the abbey of Santa Maria de Montserrat. And in that abbey is a great basilica that houses one of the most revered objects in northeastern Spain: the Virgin of Montserrat.

It's a statue of Our Lady as Queen, holding her Son the King on her lap. She holds the universe, in the form of a globe, in her right hand. This is one of the famous "Black Madonnas"—statues of Mary that have distinctive dark faces. Scholars debate endlessly why the faces are dark, and they come up with theories ranging from the perfectly reasonable (people like Mary who lived in Palestine had darker skin than people in Europe, so why shouldn't the faces be dark?) to the absurd (it's actually the Egyptian goddess Isis in disguise!). It seems as though there may be different reasons for different statues. In the case of the Virgin of Montserrat, for example, experts found that the face started out lighter and darkened over the centuries, then was repainted black. Other images were carved from wood that was dark to begin with.

The story is that this statue was carved in Jerusalem in the time of the apostles, perhaps by St. Luke (tradition says that, besides being a doctor, he was a painter and sculptor who made many images of Mary). It was hidden in a cave deep in the rocks of Montserrat as the invading Muslim armies came barreling toward northeastern Spain.

Later, in about 890, it was found again. Some shepherds heard singing and saw strange lights in the mountain. They told the priest, and the priest told the bishop, and everybody saw and heard the same thing. The strange phenomena led them to a cave where they found an image of the Blessed Virgin. But even though it was a small thing, no one could lift it.

In fact it couldn't be lifted until the bishop decided to build a chapel right near the cave. Then suddenly the statue wasn't so heavy. Thus the abbey was built around it.

As time went on, that abbey became a center for pilgrimages that was famous all over Spain and the rest of Europe. One of those pilgrims, centuries later, would change the world. When Ignatius Loyola—yes, that Saint Ignatius Loyola—experienced his religious conversion, he went to the monastery of Santa Maria de Montserrat to change his life. Then he went off and founded the Jesuits.

Pope Francis is a Jesuit.

Mary is right there again, at the crossroads of history.

There's a very similar story in the tiny mountain country of Andorra, whose patroness is Our Lady of Meritxell. Here in the late 1100s a statue was found buried under a wild rose that somehow was blooming in the middle of the winter. (Roses in the middle of the winter! Hold onto that thought, because that's going to come up later.) It became the national symbol of Andorra, the way Our Lady of the Pillar is the national symbol of Spain.

Another famous Black Madonna is at Torreciudad, which has been a pilgrimage site since at least 1084. This image is especially famous today because, more than a century ago, two loving parents promised a pilgrimage to the shrine if their dying two-year-old could recover. The doctor had given up on him and already made arrangements to pick up the body. But the boy did recover, and years later he went on to found another famous religious group that I happen to know something about: Opus Dei. Yes, the boy was St. Josemaria Escriva, and today if you go to Torreciudad you'll see the shrine that was built in gratitude for the life the Virgin of Torreciudad gave him.

And of course we can't let the subject of buried statues go without the one that was found near a river valley in the ancient province of Extremadura. There, as the Muslim armies advanced, the priests buried an image of the Virgin and Child that was said to have been carved by St.

Luke himself. The name of the river was Guadalupe, and the image is known as Our Lady of Guadalupe.

But it's not *that* Our Lady of Guadalupe. Is there a connection? Oh, yes—as we'll find out soon enough.

But we have the rest of the Middle Ages to get through first. Mary was about to intervene in history in a way that changed the life of every Catholic, including you and me personally.

Meanwhile, there's just one little story from the days of the Reconquista that I want to leave you with. It's a sweet love story. As the Christian kingdoms in the hills slowly snatched back land from the Muslims, inch-by-inch, there was a Muslim princess who fell in love with a Christian knight. He belonged to the kingdom of Portugal, which hadn't been separate from the Spanish kingdoms very long. The princess converted to Christianity and married her knight, and he took her back home to the hills of Portugal, where he loved her so dearly that he named his little town after her.

And what was her name? You can probably guess, because it was just about the most common woman's name in the Muslim world. Her name was Fatima.

5. The Flowering of Christendom

Let's set the stage here.

We're going back to the south of France in the early 1200s. It's a beautiful place, but right now it's got a problem. It's infested with heretics who are luring people away from the Church.

Bad ideas never go away. Every time I hear somebody talk about some *amazing new idea* that's going to *totally change* everything we know about Christianity, I know what it's going to be. I know it's going to be something that will make me say, "Oh, yeah, St. Irenaeus had to deal with that in the second century."

That's what was going on down here in the south of France in the early 1200s. Gnostic dualism had come out from whatever rock it had been hiding under all those years, and now it was making lots of converts.

Dualism is the idea that there are two equal principles in the world, a good one and an evil one. And it was the evil one—Satan—that created the material world. In order to reach perfection, you have to get rid of all your connection with the material world.

Needless to say, this isn't what orthodox Christians believe. Christians believe that God is the supreme power, that evil can exist only because God gives his creatures free will, that God created the universe, and that creation is very good (see Genesis 1:31). It's true that the world is broken by sin, but that doesn't mean the material world is evil.

So that brings us to Gnosticism, the other part of Gnostic dualism. Gnostics believe that there is a *secret* knowledge passed down from Jesus Christ that orthodox Christians don't have. Right. He taught one thing to the masses, because they couldn't take the truth. But *you*, the Gnostic disciple, are smart enough to learn Jesus' real teaching.

St. Irenaeus of Lyons wrote a whole book called *Against Heresies* about these people way back in the late 100s A.D. But bad ideas never go away, and here they were again. This time the Gnostic dualists were called

Cathars. To be fair to their followers, they had some reason for thinking the Cathars might be on to something. The Cathars' leaders led very simple and apparently holy lives, because they were trying to pull themselves out of the material world. (It's said that some of them just starved themselves to death, which accelerated the pulling-out process.) The Catholic clergy, I'm sorry to say, didn't always lead such holy lives. Bishops meddled in politics and led armies. Priests lived lives of luxury and kept mistresses. This isn't all of them, you understand, but it was enough of them to make a bad impression. You and I have lived through some times where the actions of a very few priests endangered the reputation of all the rest, so we can understand how that happens.

So what could be done about these heretics? Obviously the thing to do was show them that they were wrong and persuade them to come back to the Church. But that was easier said than done. A Spanish priest named Dominic set out to do exactly that. He founded an order of preachers who were to live simple and holy lives, so that anyone could see where the real holiness was.

But he wasn't getting anywhere.

Until Our Lady intervened.

The traditional story is that she appeared to Dominic in 1206. She had a suggestion. Dominic should teach people a simple and engaging way of praying. They would intersperse praying the Hail Mary with contemplations of the mysteries of salvation. Every time they prayed, they'd be remembering the facts of the Catholic faith. And they could keep track of their prayers on a string of beads like this—

And she handed him a rosary.

It was like a bomb going off in medieval culture—a bomb that exploded in a shower of roses. The rest of the 1200s was one of the most amazingly creative ages in the history of humanity. Just let me rattle off some things practically at random. Saint Francis of Assisi. Saint Bonaventure. Saint Thomas Aquinas. Saint Louis of France. The building of the great cathedrals—Notre Dame, Chartres, Orvieto. The building of Mont-Saint-Michel. The height of Christian philosophy.

It was a peak in Christian worship, too, and we're still mining its riches. The Mass for Corpus Christi. Thomas Aquinas' famous hymn *Pange Lingua*. His *Tantum Ergo* that has become part of our Eucharistic liturgy. His *O Salutaris Hostia*. These classics are standards in our worship today—and they come to us from that glorious explosion of culture 800 years ago.

And it all started with Our Lady appearing to St. Dominic and giving him the Rosary. That's not just a key moment in the history of Christianity. It's a key moment in the history of Western civilization.

We've only got time to hit the highlights here. But what highlights they are!

You'd have to be crazy

Think of St. Francis, for example—the saint whose name Pope Francis decided to take. Even today his name stands for everything a Christian ought to be.

You've probably heard the story of how Francis was a rich young wastrel who spent all his time partying, but he had a conversion experience in prison and gave up everything—even the clothes on his back.

That was pretty amazing on its own. But where he really started to change history was when he heard the Gospel preached and decided to take it seriously.

You've heard the story many times. It's in the tenth chapter of Matthew's Gospel. Jesus sends the Twelve out to preach, and he tells them not to take anything with them.

> As you go, make this proclamation: "The kingdom of heaven is at hand." Cure the sick, raise the dead, cleanse lepers, drive out demons. Without cost you have received; without cost you are to give. Do not take gold or silver or copper for your belts; no sack for the journey, or a second tunic, or sandals, or walking stick. The laborer deserves his keep. [Matthew 10:7-10.]

Jesus usually meant what he said, didn't he? And we know that we have the same job the disciples had: to take the Good News out into the world and preach it to everyone.

So if we were to take Jesus' instructions *really* seriously, we'd give up everything and just walk out and preach, trusting that people would give us enough to survive.

But we wouldn't do that, because you'd have to be crazy to do that.

But Francis—well, maybe he was a little bit crazy. But he was the kind of crazy that gets things done. And he decided that, if Jesus had given his disciples those instructions, then he must have meant what he said.

That was the beginning of the Franciscans—an order founded on the idea that its members would have no possessions whatsoever, but would trust in the generosity of the people they preached to.

And where was St. Francis when he had this sudden revelation?

He was in the chapel of St. Mary of the Angels. And as a matter of fact, it happened right after St. Dominic's encounter with the Blessed Mother.

There she is again—Mary, standing at the crossroads of history, giving Francis a little shove in the right direction.

So Francis became the leader of a movement. And that movement would soon inspire another saint to bring one of the Catholic world's favorite prayers to the masses.

The Angelus

The Franciscans—the movement St. Francis had founded—used to say three Hail Marys every evening when they heard the bell for Compline, the service at the end of the day.

But why should it be just the Franciscans? That was the question St. Bonaventure asked himself.

Bonaventure had known St. Francis himself. As a child, Bonaventure had been very sick, and when he was taken to St. Francis he got better.

After a miraculous cure like that, Bonaventure knew what he wanted to be when he grew up.

He joined the Franciscans when he was a young man, and by his middle thirties he was in charge of the whole order. Even in his lifetime, Bonaventure was recognized as one of the most important figures in the Church. The pope looked to him for advice.

And that was how Bonaventure came to suggest that maybe everybody could do what the Franciscans did: they could stop everything and pray a short prayer when they heard the Compline bell.

We call the prayer the Angelus after its first word in Latin: *Angelus Domini nuntiavit Mariae*—"The Angel of the Lord declared unto Mary". It became a traditional marker of the time all over Europe: when the bell rang, evening was here, and everything stopped for a moment. Farmers stopped in the fields and bowed their heads. Travelers stopped along the road. Merchants stopped bickering with customers, and both recited the prayer together. Soon there was a morning Angelus, too, and then a midday bell. Prayers marked the beginning, the middle, and the end of the working day.

That wasn't Bonaventure's only accomplishment, of course. He was a famous theologian even in his own time, and some people think of him as the second-greatest teacher of the Middle Ages.

Second-greatest?

Yes, second, because he came from a very talented class at the University of Paris. One of his classmates was a big fellow who didn't say much. But eventually he would have quite a bit to say.

The Dumb Ox

Thomas Aquinas just might have been the most systematic philosopher who ever lived. Yet his schoolmates at the University of Paris thought he would never amount to anything. They called him "the dumb ox." (Do you suppose his classmate Bonaventure ever called him that? Probably not.) His professor Albert—we call him Albertus Magnus, Albert the Great—told the young men, "We call this young man a dumb ox, but his bellowing in doctrine will one day resound throughout the world."

And he was right. Kids, if you're voted "least likely to succeed," don't despair. People often don't recognize talent. You might be another Aquinas.

Thomas was another gift that came out of St. Dominic's encounter with Our Lady. He had joined Dominic's new order of preachers. And he took his job very seriously.

He had a bit of luck: it was just about this time that the works of the Greek philosopher Aristotle started to filter into Europe—translated by those Christians who were still living under Muslim domination in Spain. You remember how they managed to take the little bits of Greek and Roman culture that were still floating around in the Caliphate and put them into Latin so Western Europeans could understand them. Now their labors bore fruit, and bore it in abundance. Aristotle taught Thomas how to use logic to make arguments you couldn't wiggle out from under. And Thomas put that skill to work to place all of Christian doctrine on a sound logical basis.

His massive *Summa Theologica* is a complete compendium of everything there is to know about the Catholic Christian faith. But it's not just big catechism that tells you what you need to believe. It tells you exactly why what we believe is *true*. Thomas works the whole faith out logically—and he does it by giving the opponents of the faith the fairest possible hearing.

For example, Thomas tackles the question of the Real Presence in the Eucharist: "Whether the body of Christ be in this sacrament in very truth, or merely as in a figure or sign?"

Immediately he starts with "Objection 1. It seems that the body of Christ is not in this sacrament in very truth, but only as in a figure, or sign. For it is written that..." And then he goes on to give the very best scriptural argument for that position. And there are three more "objections" to come. "Objection 3. Further, no body can be in several places at the one time. For this does not even belong to an angel; since for the same reason it could be everywhere. But Christ's is a true body..."

Whatever arguments the Protestants would think of three hundred years later, Thomas had already thought of them. His whole system works only because he gives his opponents the very best arguments they could come up with, and usually expresses them better than they could have expressed them. And then comes Aquinas with "I answer that..." And he carefully answers each argument and shows that the Catholic position is the only one a reasonable person could accept.

So naturally he applies the same inescapable logic to the questions that come up about Mary. For example: "Whether Christ's Mother remained a virgin after his birth?"

Here come the "objections." "It would seem that Christ's Mother did not remain a virgin after His Birth. For it is written: 'Before Joseph and Mary came together, she was found with child of the Holy Ghost' (see Matthew 1:18). Now the Evangelist would not have said this—'before they came together'—unless he were certain of their subsequent coming together; for no one says of one who does not eventually dine 'before he dines.'" And another objection: "Further, 'first-born' can only be said of one who has brothers afterwards..." And of course there are the "brothers" of Jesus mentioned in Scripture. Once again, every argument a Protestant could think of, St. Thomas Aquinas already thought of it.

But what is the truth? It's heresy to say that Christ's mother was not a virgin after his birth. "We must therefore simply assert that the Mother of God, as she was a virgin in conceiving him and a virgin in giving him birth, did she remain a virgin ever afterwards."

All the objections have reasonable answers. You can find many examples of somebody saying "before this happened, I did that"—so that the second thing prevented the first from ever happening. You can find elsewhere in Scripture that "first-born" means the child who was born first, even if no other children were born afterwards. "Brothers" is used in four different senses in Scripture (it's typical of St. Thomas to classify the senses so carefully), and here it means people of the same family, but not with the same mother and father. And so on.[7]

This is what makes the *Summa Theologica* such a towering landmark of human thought: St. Thomas carefully examines everything—even the life of Mary and Jesus—in the light of reason, leaving no need or room for doubt.

So reason reached a peak in the high Middle Ages. But so did Christian mysticism. Where St. Thomas reasoned his way to devotion to Mary, other great saints focused on the mystical experience of the love of Christ and his Mother.

Love drove a woman named Juliana to push every Church authority she knew to celebrate a feast in honor of the Blessed Sacrament.

Orvieto and Corpus Christi

St. Juliana of Mont Cornillon was a nun who had always been devoted to the Eucharist, and her fondest desire was to see the Church celebrate a feast in its honor. Now, a lot of people want to make improvements in the Church. I could suggest a few. But Juliana had a gift for making friends, and she got the local bishop on her side. She also told her idea to the archdeacon Jacques Pantaléon, which turned out to be a good idea, because he was on the pope track.

Juliana didn't live long enough to see it, but her friend Jacques did become Pope—Pope Urban IV. Somewhere in the back of his mind, he still had that idea she had planted in his brain about a feast in honor of the Blessed Sacrament. But he didn't do anything about it until something happened to jog his memory.

Orvieto is an ancient city outside Rome. When I say *ancient,* I mean really, really old. The ancient Romans called it Urbs Vetus, meaning "the old city," which is where the Italian name Orvieto comes from. It was ancient to *them.* It's a wonderful place, very picturesque, with narrow streets of tile-roofed houses, and a famous wine from the nearby hills. It's easy to see why it was a favorite residence of the popes in the Middle

---

[7]   Thomas Aquinas, *Summa Theologica,* Third Part, Question 28, Article 3.

Ages, and Pope Urban IV lived there for most of his reign. And the town's cathedral houses a wonderful relic.

In 1263, the tradition says, a priest in the little village of Bolsena outside Orvieto was having doubts. He just couldn't bring himself to believe that the Eucharist was really the Body and Blood of Jesus.

Until the host he had consecrated started to bleed.

Drops of blood fell on the corporal, the cloth under the host, and the priest's doubts were gone.

Word of the miracle spread quickly, and the pope heard of it at Orvieto. It just so happened that Thomas Aquinas, who you'll remember had one of the greatest minds in the history of the Church, was living in Orvieto at the time. With Thomas backing him up, the pope finally gave the whole Church the feast St. Juliana had wished for.

Not long after, the people of Orvieto started building their proudest monument: a cathedral that now houses that blood-stained corporal from Bolsena.

Devotion in stone

What's the first image that comes to mind when you think of the glories of the Middle Ages? For almost everyone, it would be a great Gothic cathedral like the one in Orvieto, or like York Minster or Chartres. More of them were dedicated to Our Lady than to anyone else, of course—Notre-Dame in Paris is one example everybody remembers, and the one in Chartres is dedicated to Notre-Dame ("Our Lady"), too.

Even today these cathedrals strike awe into everyone who walks into them. Imagine how they must have struck people when they were new. Older churches had been dim places, because the stonework needed to support the large structures had to be thick and heavy, and that didn't leave a lot of space for windows. Just think of the engineering work that had to be done to solve that problem! But nothing was too difficult if it was for the glory of God. No work was too much work if it was done out of love for Our Lady. And so great minds set to work to solve the problem: how can we make a church building worthy of the love and devo-tion we feel? How can we translate our praise into stone?

Master builders directed the projects, but these cathedrals were never the work of one person. It wasn't like today, where an architect draws a building on a sheet of paper (or in a CAD program) and tells a builder, "Make that." When a great cathedral was going up, every craft in the city was involved. Every piece of the work was made to glorify God and to praise the Blessed Mother. You can see the results in the stained glass, the marvelous carvings everywhere, the statues on the façade. But workers restoring cathedrals are sometimes astonished to go up into the invisible rafters and find carvings in the wood where no one could possibly see them. No one could see—but Our Lady would know that some devoted craftsman did his best work for her.

Glorious cathedrals rose all over Europe. But there's a special concen-tration of them in France. And some of that was because, for a while, France had a saint for a king.

The king who was a saint

Now, when was the last time you heard of a king who was a saint? Think of our world leaders today. Which one of them do you expect to end up with a place on the Church calendar?

I can't think of one either.

But Louis IX is such a famous saint that the French named a big city in Missouri after him.

What made Louis a saint?

Well, he did saintly things. He let beggars eat from the king's table, and *he* ate what was left over from the *beggars'* dinners. He built hospitals and homes for women who had been prostitutes ("Daughters of God," he called them). He helped lepers—and I don't mean he appointed a commission to hire bureaucrats to study the feasibility of establishing a committee to appoint administrators to oversee the construction of a multimillion-franc research institute. I mean King Louis went and tended to the lepers himself, with his own hands.

Of course he was a big patron of the arts, because in those days the arts meant things to embellish the Church. That's one of the reasons France is stuffed with great Gothic cathedrals to this day.

One other thing St. Louis did was to go off on crusades, and I probably need to explain something about the Crusades, because I think most of us have the wrong idea about the Crusades these days.

The Crusades: what really happened

I think the dominant narrative about the Crusades has become that a bunch of Christians went over and attacked the Muslims without any provocation at all. And that's just not the way it happened.

But before I summarize the history of that period, I need to say that I have the highest respect for Muslims, a number of whom were my students during my years at Northridge Prep. They have respect for the Ten Commandments, traditional marriage, pro-life values, and zeal for God. Muslims were key allies with the Vatican at the Beijing World Conference on Women in 1995 and the International Conference on Population and Development in Cairo in 1994. Still, our religious convictions differ on the nature of God and the Holy Trinity, and that has consequences. But back to the period of the Crusades and the Blessed Mother's intervention in human history.

The important thing to know is that what brought on the Crusades wasn't Christians hating Muslims or vice versa. It was a regime change in the Middle East.

You remember that the Arab armies had conquered most of the East way back in the 600s. That included the Holy Land, of course—which is holy to Muslims, too.

For a long time, the Muslim rulers had been reasonably tolerant in the Holy Land. The Christians who lived there were allowed to go about their business, and the thousands of pilgrims who came to see the holy sites were welcome. But at some time in the 1070s, Seljuk Turks under Tutush or Toucush became masters of Jerusalem and the holy sites. Where the previous government had had a well-organized program of fees and rules for Christian pilgrims, the new rulers started just kidnapping them on the highway and shaking them down for cash. Now a trip to the Holy Land meant taking your life in your hands. And the new rulers didn't treat their own Christian subjects any better. They broke up Masses and smashed sacred images. They tore down churches. They grabbed the Patriarch of Jerusalem by his hair and physically dragged him off to a cell, then demanded a huge ransom to let him out.

Meanwhile, there was serious trouble for the Byzantine Empire—you remember, the remaining half of the Roman Empire that had never fallen, although it did a lot of declining. The Turks had conquered most of Anatolia—the land that, not coincidentally, we call Turkey today. Anatolia had been the richer half of the Empire, which was now confined mostly to today's Greece. And so the emperor took an extraordinary step: he asked the West for help.

This was the background of the Crusades. I'm not going to get into the Crusades very deeply, because a whole book about the Crusades would hardly scratch the surface. And I'm certainly not going to say that everything every Christian did in the Crusades was good. But what I want to make clear is that the Crusades weren't just about a bunch of Christians deciding, "Let's go beat up some Muslims." No, the crusaders had heard the pilgrims' tales of abuse. They had heard what was happening to the Christians in Jerusalem and Syria and the rest of the Middle East. They had heard that the Roman Emperor of the East himself was in deep trouble, so deep that he was asking for help from the West.

These people heard their fellow Christians calling for help.

As we all know, the Crusades did not take the Holy Land away from the Muslims permanently. But that doesn't mean they had no lasting effect. The meeting of East and West had deep effects on European culture.

The Carmelites, for example, are a Western Catholic order named for Mount Carmel, the mountain where Elijah challenged the prophets of Baal (see 1 Kings 18). That's where they got their start, during the time when Mount Carmel was held by the Crusaders. And it seems that Our Lady picked the Carmelites for a special mission in history.

Once again, we go back to the 1200s. As the Crusades were beginning to go badly for the Western Europeans, the Carmelites decided they had to move away from Palestine. They ended up concentrated in England, and an Englishman named Simon became their prior general, the leader of the whole order. He was already very old, but he had about twenty good active years left in him—he was about a hundred when he died.

When things were going badly for the Carmelites, St. Simon Stock had a vision of Our Lady in which she was holding the brown scapular—the distinctive habit of the Carmelites. "This shall be a privilege for you and for all the Carmelites," she said: "whoever dies in this habit will be saved."

This was too good a privilege to be confined to the Carmelites. Members of the order started to confer the scapular on their friends and supporters, so that they could share in the promised privilege. It became a worldwide devotion—a marker of Our Lady's special protection. I suspect many of my readers are wearing the brown scapular right now. And we haven't heard the last of it in our story.

Meanwhile, the world that had been broadened by the Crusades was due to get a whole lot broader. Europeans were about to run into a world that had never heard the Gospel before—a world that didn't even show up on their maps.

6. Meeting of the Worlds

What happened in 1492?

You learned that poem in grade school:

"In Fourteen Hundred and Ninety-Two, Columbus sailed the ocean blue."

And *why* did Columbus sail the ocean blue in Fourteen Hundred and Ninety-Two? To discover new trade routes to the Indies?

That what we were always taught. But it took me years to discover that common narrative is "fake news," or at least a popular interpretation that does not seem to be based on facts or the historical records.

Now let me tell you the truth about Columbus. It had nothing to do with finding new trade routes to the Indies.

Read his log. It begins *In nomine Domini Jesu Christi*—which means "In the name of the Lord Jesus Christ."

That's not how you begin a business journal in Latin.

Columbus had heard about the trip Marco Polo took to China. He had heard that the Great Khan had been interested in Christianity and wanted missionaries sent to tell him more. But there hadn't been enough missionaries mad enough to go out there—especially since the places between Spain and China had gotten a lot more hostile after Marco Polo's time.

So Columbus set sail in 1492 to see if the people of Asia were open to Christianity. It had taken 781 years to recover Spain from the infidel, and now at last it was time for Mary's prophecy to Saint James to start coming true. Spain was going to take the faith all over the world.

So he named his flagship the Santa Maria.

And the winds began to blow on Saturday, September 8—the birthday of Our Lady.   And a Saturday as well, which is always dedicated to Our Lady.

There she is again. Mary at the crossroads of history.

I discover Columbus

So how did I get intrigued by Christopher Columbus?

I've always been interested in history, especially American and local history. I got my Bachelors in History as an undergrad, and usually am reading a couple of books at a time on history. But every once in a while I came across something that really grabbed my imagination. That's how I started to get into history: all the little stories that took root in my imagination.

Once I heard a story that during Columbus' voyage his sailors were at the point of despair because they were stuck in the middle of the Atlantic in the doldrums literally going nowhere. They could not go forward and they could not go back. And they had passed the point of no return.

You hear the word "doldrums" these days and usually think of an emotional state, right? You say, "I'm in the doldrums," and you mean that you feel like you just don't care anymore, like you're not going anywhere. You might not even have known that it came from a nautical term.

Well, in the ocean, the doldrums are a real thing. Meteorologists call it the Intertropical Convergence Zone, because "doldrums" is way too short to sound like science. But sailors still call it the doldrums. It's a band in the tropics where the wind dies down and the sun seems to shine forever and you just sit in your ship, stuck, because your sails are just hanging limp.

Sailors dreaded the doldrums more than they dreaded storms. At least in a storm you could do something to try to keep your ship safe. In the doldrums it was just endless waiting, wondering whether the wind would ever pick up. And every sailor had heard about the ships that didn't make it—the ships that got becalmed so long that their crews ran out of water. One of the most famous passages in one of the most famous poems in the English language is about the doldrums:

> Day after day, day after day,
>   We stuck, nor breath nor motion,

> As idle as a painted Ship
>> Upon a painted Ocean.
>
> Water, water, every where
>> And all the boards did shrink;
> Water, water, every where,
>> Nor any drop to drink.[8]

This was where Columbus and his three ships were stuck on their way west. You can imagine what the crew was thinking. They probably thought Columbus was crazy anyway, because only a madman would go west to get to the East. And now they were stuck in the doldrums, thinking, "We're lost! We can't go back, we can't go forward, what's going to happen to us? We're all going to die out here!"

And this is the story I had heard: to encourage these sailors, Columbus used to gather them all together on the deck of his ship in the evening as the sun was going down, and they would sing the Salve Regina to regain their hope.

I thought it was a beautiful story. But was it true? Too many perfect stories turn out not to be true.

So I went looking for evidence of it. I looked all over the Internet, and at last I came upon a copy of Columbus' travel log. And just the first page of it really grabbed me.

It turns out the Salve Regina wasn't the only thing religious about his voyage. In fact it was religious from beginning to end.

Now, this thing I found is not quite his original log. That's been lost for a long time. But two people copied large parts of the log before it was lost. One of them was his son, and one of them was the historian Bartolomé de Las Casas, who copied a lot of it for his *General History of the Indies*. Some of it he just summarized, but he copied a good bit verbatim. And one of the verbatim parts happens to be the preamble or introduc-

---

[8] Samuel Taylor Coleridge, "The Rime of the Ancient Mariner," in *Lyrical Ballads* by W. Wordsworth.

tion, where Columbus explains why he wanted to go to the East in the first place.

Why did Columbus set out on his voyage? Right here at the beginning of the log, he makes it as clear as anyone could want.

Why Columbus sailed

Columbus had been there when the city of Granada, the last Muslim holdout in Spain, was surrendered to Isabella and Ferdinand. "I saw the royal banners of Your Highnesses placed on the towers of the Alhambra, which is the fortress of that city, and I saw the Moorish king come forth from the gates of the city and kiss the royal hands of your Highnesses, and of the Prince my lord," he tells the king and queen (the whole log is addressed to them).

And apparently Columbus had an opportunity at the time to convey an important fact to their Majesties, because he says that in response to that important fact, they agreed to sponsor his voyage: "and presently in that same month, acting on the information that I had given to your Highnesses touching the lands of India, and respecting a prince called the Great Khan, which means in our language King of Kings, how he and his ancestors had sent to Rome many times to ask for learned men of our holy faith to teach him, and how the Holy Father had never complied, insomuch that many people believing in idolatries were lost by receiving doctrine of perdition"—

Well, Columbus uses a lot of long sentences, which is what you do when you're talking to royalty. But the upshot of it all is this: Isabella and Ferdinand were sending him to the Indies (which vaguely included everything from India to China and whatever else might be out there) because there were people there who needed to hear the Good News.

Now, where did he get that idea?

Well, it turns out we know exactly where Columbus got his information. It was from Marco Polo. Remember him? He was the Venetian traveler who went all the way to China about 200 years before Columbus sailed to America. Columbus owned a copy of Marco Polo's *Travels*. And right there where it talks about the Khan sending ambassadors to the pope, there's a note in the margin in Columbus' own handwriting: "The Great Khan sent ambassadors to the pontiff."[9]

He wrote that summary because he wanted to remember that passage. It was important to him.

So that's where he got his information. And that's why he wanted to go to the East so desperately. There was unfinished business there. People were wandering in the darkness. We were losing them by the millions, because nobody had brought them the Gospel.

In case you didn't get it just by reading Columbus' own words, the editor of the translation I was reading adds a footnote. "It is interesting to notice the emphasis of the missionary motive in this preamble. Nothing is said in regard to the search for a new route to the Indies for commercial reasons."[10]

Yeah, that *is* interesting, isn't it? It's not exactly the way we usually hear the story.

And it sort of made me wonder: What else had I been missing in the story of Columbus?

The secret patron

That was when I started connecting the dots. The whole story of Columbus is amazing! It's as though everything that happened was under the patronage of Our Lady.

First of all, when did he set sail? He made it to the Canary Islands, which were already a Spanish possession. But there was no wind. The winds didn't start to blow until September 8—the Nativity of Our Lady, and a Saturday. Then suddenly there was exactly the wind he needed coming out of the northeast. A week later, on September 15, the Feast of Our Lady of Sorrows, Columbus reported seeing a "large branch of fire falling from the sky into the sea some twenty leagues distant." On the

---

[9] "Magnus Kam misit legatos ad pontificem." *The Northmen, Columbus, and Cabot*, p. 89, note 2.

[10] *The Northmen, Columbus, and Cabot*, p. 90, note 1.

verge of an extraordinary event—Europe's discovery of the New World —there was celestial, a cosmological augur in the sky. Just like what happened in the sky with the Star of David before Our Lord's birth. Like the celestial wonder seen by the sailors of Don Juan en route to Lepanto in 1571, and like the terrible omen of the Aurora Borealis in January, 1938, known as the "Fatima Storm," presaging the terrible Kristallnacht and Blitzkrieg soon to follow that started the horrible Second World War. But I digress. So back to the story of Columbus and his maiden voyage.

On October 11—just after the crew had sung the *Salve Regina,* by the way, the hymn to Mary we know as "Hail, Holy Queen"—the fleet first sighted land. October 11 was the feast of Mary, Mother of God, in the church calendar of the time. (Now celebrated on January 1.)

But it wasn't till the next day that they set foot on the shore.

That's what we call Columbus Day—October 12. That was the day Columbus and his crew first landed on the soil of the New World.

And what day was October 12 *for Columbus?*

It's the feast of Our Lady of the Pillar.

You remember that from way back at the beginning of the story? St. James the apostle was in Spain, about to give up. And the Blessed Mother appeared to him—even though she was alive and well at the other end of the Mediterranean—and told him, "Look, I know you're having a tough time. But stick with it, because if you convert these Spanish people, they'll take the faith all over the world."

The feast of Our Lady of the Pillar is a big day in Spain. In fact, it's now the national holiday of Spain—their equivalent of our American July 4. In the time of Columbus, it was especially a big deal in Aragon, which is where King Ferdinand came from. "Spain" was not really a country yet: it was two kingdoms, Aragon and Castile, whose queen and king happened to be married.

And here's Columbus, landing in a part of the world that had never heard the Gospel, precisely on the feast of Our Lady of the Pillar.

There she is again! Mary at the crossroads of history. I should write a book about this stuff.

And where did Columbus go when he got back from his first voyage? He went on a pilgrimage to a sacred site that meant a lot to him.

It seems there was a terrific storm on the way back, and Columbus had told his men to pray to Our Lady for deliverance. But they did more than pray. Columbus decided that, if they survived the storm, one of them would make a pilgrimage to the shrine of Our Lady of Guadalupe in Spain. They would draw lots to see which one it would be.

So they took some dry chickpeas out of the stores, and on one of them they cut a cross. Then they dropped them in a hat. The one who drew out the chickpea with the cross would be the one to make the pilgrimage.

Columbus, as the commander, put in his hand first—and drew out the one with the cross.[11]

And that was why when he got back to Spain, Columbus went to thank Our Lady of Guadalupe. He had promised to pay a visit to thank her for delivering them from the storm.

But Columbus had another reason to be grateful, too. It wasn't his first pilgrimage there. And it was while he was on his first pilgrimage to Our Lady of Guadalupe that he met with representatives from Ferdinand and Isabella—an encounter that ultimately led to his meeting the king and queen themselves, which led to his trip to the Indies. That was why he had picked Our Lady of Guadalupe as the shrine for the pilgrimage.

There she is again: Mary at the crossroads of history.

Columbus made three more trips west, always believing he was going to the East Indies, never realizing that he had discovered a part of the world Europeans hadn't even heard of. And wherever Columbus went, he thought of Mary—and, of course, of her Son. The first island he came to he called San Salvador, Holy Savior in English. The second he called Santa Maria de la Concepcion—Saint Mary of the Conception.

Of course he thought of Mary especially in her connection with Spain, his sponsor. Columbus sighted one small island with a tall mountain in

---

[11] Columbus' journal, in *The Northmen, Columbus, and Cabot,* p. 239.

the middle of it, and he named it Montserrat, after the Virgin of Montserrat back home in Spain. It's still called Montserrat today.

He gave the name Guadalupe to another bigger island that he sighted on his second voyage. It still bears the name today, though in the French spelling—Guadeloupe.

But how about that mission of his? How did it go? Was Columbus successful in bringing the Gospel to the Indies?

Mixed reviews

Well, let's leave out the part about his not being where he thought he was. He found a world full of people who had never heard the Gospel before. Did he succeed in bringing them the Good News?

I think we'd have to say the story is complicated. Columbus himself was human, so he wasn't perfect. Neither was his crew.

I do think the people who get hysterical every Columbus Day and accuse him of genocide are a little misguided. We fail to understand the context of history if we read it through the prism of modern and contemporary sensibilities.

But actually, if you don't know the history, you might believe the same things. It definitely is true that a huge number of people died after the first European contact with America. Most of them died from European diseases, and unless you got in a time machine and went back to explain germ theory to the people of Renaissance Europe, there's not much they could have done to prevent that. They had no way of knowing that the diseases they survived would wipe out whole populations. Columbus thought his crew were pretty healthy specimens, and the Indies were a healthy place. "I thank our Lord that, up to this time, there has not been a person of my company who has had so much as a headache, or been in bed from illness, except an old man who has suffered from the stone all his life, and he was well again in two days."[12]

So it's compressing a lot of history and leaving out a good bit to make Columbus responsible for the epidemics that wiped out so many people

---

[12] Columbus' journal, in *The Northmen, Columbus, and Cabot,* p. 160.

in the Americas. But epidemics did happen, and no one can diminish the suffering they caused. If we were meeting people from a new world today, I hope we'd be more aware of the germs we carried and take more care. As I said, though, without knowing how germs work, there wasn't much Europeans could do about their diseases.

It's helpful to remember that European diseases also decimated European populations in the Middle Ages: the black death, the bubonic plague. And to be fair and balanced in our calculation of history, who benefitted more from this transatlantic cultural exchange? Europe or America? Europe got chocolate from America, and America got coffee from Europe!!

But back to the story about Columbus.

What about his relations with the people he met on the islands, though?

Columbus was sure those encounters would go well. He hadn't been able to see much yet, he wrote after a few weeks in the Caribbean.

> But now, if our Lord pleases, I will see as much as possible, and will proceed by little and little, learning and comprehending; and I will make some of my followers learn the language. For I have perceived that there is only one language up to this point. After they understand the advantages, I shall labor to make all these people Christians. They will become so readily, because they have no religion nor idolatry, and your Highnesses will send orders to build a city and fortress, and to convert the people.[13]

And in another passage,

> I hold, most serene Princes, that if devout religious persons were here, knowing the language, they would all turn Christian. I trust in the Lord that your Highnesses will resolve upon

---

[13] Columbus' journal, in *The Northmen, Columbus, and Cabot*, p. 159-160.

this with much diligence, to bring so many great nations within the Church, and to convert them..."[14]

Obviously he was sticking to his original plan. He would bring the Gospel to the Indies, and of course the people would accept it eagerly.

Was that naive? Well, yes, it was—as we know now. But Columbus was naive. And I mean that in a good way. He wanted to believe the best of the people he met.

And you know what? Usually he was right. For weeks he went from island to island in the Caribbean, and the worst thing that happened was that some of the natives ran away in terror from the strange men who came in monstrously huge boats. Just as often he met the people on the islands and made friends. They seemed like nice places, these Indies.

But he did hear stories from these people about other people who were not so nice. He noticed that some of the islanders had scars, and they told him—as well as they could, given the language barrier—that there were other people on other islands who came to take people away. Caribs was the name they gave to these people—a name that gives us our name for the Caribbean Sea. But there were awful stories about them: their name has given us our word "cannibal," too.

I think Columbus abused the trust of the people he met when he forced some of them to come with him to go back to Spain. I think he thought he was doing them a favor, but I don't know that *they* saw it that way.

Columbus did have one altercation with well-armed natives on that first voyage, but on the whole he had good encounters with most of the people he met. He was not always so lucky on the other voyages, and when he became governor of the colonies he founded he showed that he was not cut out to be a governor at all. He didn't know how to maintain order without tyranny.

But Columbus, though he had human faults, was not responsible for genocide.

---

[14] Columbus' journal, in *The Northmen, Columbus, and Cabot*, p. 142.

Where the real tragedy started to happen was when people who were more motivated by greed started coming out from Spain to pick up all this gold they had heard was lying around on the ground in the New World.

Some of the Spanish colonists made slaves out of the people who were there before them, with no justification other than greed. There were massacres and wars. Greedy adventurers came and conquered people who were in no position to resist. We know about all the massacres, tortures, and brutality because of that same historian who preserved what we have of Columbus' journal, Bartolomé de Las Casas. He was incandescently furious at the way some of his countrymen were treating the people they conquered, and he spent much of his life trying to make the Spanish government do something about it. He succeeded, too—but only insofar as the Spanish government could control what was going on in the New World.

That was what the extraordinarily courageous friars—like Las Casas—who came to convert the people of the New World had to deal with. They made some converts, because some people could see that the friars were living a life of real selflessness and dedication. But the conversions weren't piling up the way Columbus had hoped. It just didn't seem humanly possible to make the New World Christian.

And it probably wasn't.

But Our Lady has never confined herself to what was humanly possible.

The world of Juan Diego

Now, at last, we come to the most important date in the last thousand years. But to set you up for it, let me tell you about the world it happened in.

Mexico was the land where some of the most sophisticated civilizations of the New World had developed. They built huge temples and magnificent works of architecture. They organized vast numbers of people and built enormous cities. Some of them invented sophisticated systems of writing independent from anything in the Old World.

And one thing all these civilizations seem to have had in common was human sacrifice.

The gods needed blood—human blood.

And no one was better at giving it to them than the Aztecs.

The Aztecs did everything big. Their capital city, Tenochtitlan (today's Mexico City), was possibly the biggest city in the world at the time. It was certainly bigger than any city anyone from Spain had seen. It was filled with enormous public buildings and palaces and temples.

And, of course, those temples needed a lot of human sacrifices.

In fact, the need for human sacrifices was one of the main things that drove the Aztecs to build an empire. It's all very well to sacrifice people to the gods, but wouldn't you rather have it be *other* people? So the Aztecs conquered other people, and then forced them to provide huge numbers of human sacrifices.

And when I say huge numbers, I mean numbers like you wouldn't believe. According to the Aztecs' own historians, they sacrificed tens of thousands of victims at the dedication of one temple alone. You could compare these human sacrifices to the horrible genocides of the Second World War.

As I said, the Aztecs did everything big. I would describe things in more detail, but your stomach couldn't take it. You couldn't read a paragraph about the horrors of that degraded civilization. You could not stomach the descriptions of what actually happened. At least I couldn't, so if you want the details, look them up on Wikipedia, because I'm not going to go there.

In 1519, a Spanish adventurer named Cortés showed up with a few hundred men in some stolen ships, and in a short time he had conquered the whole Aztec Empire.

That's the way we usually hear the story. But that way of telling it leaves out one important fact. The reason Cortés was able to succeed was that he had about a hundred thousand other Mexicans behind him who were sick of the Aztecs and thought practically anybody would be better. And you can bet the endless demand for human sacrifices was part of that resentment.

So you'd think the people in Mexico would be ready to embrace Christianity, just because it gave them a rest from all the sacrifices. But Cortés and his Spanish troops turned out to be nearly as bad as the Aztecs. The usual catalogue of cruelty and injustice followed.

But there were, as always, dedicated missionaries who did their best to spread the Gospel even in such adverse conditions. And they did make a few converts.

One of them was a man named Juan Diego.

Roses in the winter

Juan Diego was born before Columbus sailed, and he led an unremarkable life. No one really expected great things from him. But he had converted to the Catholic faith, and he took it seriously. He always showed up for Mass and his catechism lessons.

One day in 1531—just twelve years after the conquest—he was walking past Tepayac Hill out in the country not far from Mexico City when a beautiful lady surrounded by light appeared to him. She was the Mother of God, she said, and she had a favor to ask of him. Could he ask the bishop to build her a chapel there? That way anyone who was having troubles could come and ask for her help.

Would you be surprised to hear that the bishop didn't believe Juan Diego? And you have to be fair to him. You probably wouldn't have believed the story, either.

Poor Juan Diego went back and forth between the Lady and the bishop, and finally the bishop told him he needed to ask for a sign. If he could bring some sign to prove it was really Our Lady who was talking to him, then the bishop would believe him.

The Lady promised Juan Diego that she would have a sign for him the next day. But Juan Diego didn't show up the next day. His uncle had become terribly ill, and Juan Diego had to sit by his bedside and tend to the poor man.

The day after that, when it looked as though his uncle was about to die, Juan Diego decided he had to go for a priest to take the old man's last confession. Once again Our Lady met him. Juan Diego apologized for missing her two days before, but his uncle was sick, and...

"Am I not here, who am your mother?" the Lady asked. She could take care of everything if he would just put his faith in her. As a matter of fact, he could stop worrying about his uncle. And he could take that sign to the bishop. If he would just go up the hill to where they had met before, he could pick some flowers there.

It was the middle of the winter, but Juan Diego found beautiful roses blooming just where she said they would be.

Roses in the middle of the winter! It seems to be a sign that follows the Blessed Mother wherever she goes.

Juan Diego picked as many as he could carry and wrapped them up in his cloak. When he got to the bishop (who kept him waiting, because he was nobody important), Juan Diego dumped the roses out of his cloak on the floor.

And there, on the inside of the cloak, was a perfect image of the Lady Juan Diego had met.

The day was December 12—which we celebrate now as the feast of Our Lady of Guadalupe. Because that was what Our Lady told Juan Diego to call her: Our Lady of Guadalupe—the same name by which she had been the special friend of Columbus on his voyage.

But wait! Do you know what day it *actually* was?

I ask that because there was a little hiccup in the calendar. Do you know the difference between the Julian calendar and the Gregorian calendar? Well, I'm about to tell you, whether you know it or not.

Calendar drift

Julius Caesar reformed the calendar in 46 B.C., and he did a great job. (Mostly because he wasn't the one who did the actual work: he had

Greek mathematicians and astronomers for that. Perhaps Aristarchus of Samos, three centuries before Christ, had already made the calculations.)

We have two basic phenomena to worry about in a calendar: days and years. The problem to solve when you're making the calendar is that the solar year doesn't divide evenly into days. It's about 365 and a quarter days long. So the Julian calendar (you get to name all kinds of things after yourself when you're dictator for life) solved that problem by having 365 days and adding an extra day every four years. Simple and really, really accurate. When I say accurate, I mean that the Julian calendar was accurate to less than eleven minutes per year. That's pretty darn good!

Until a lot of years go by. Then those minutes start to add up. And you start to find that the seasons aren't happening quite when they're supposed to happen.

Pope Gregory XIII introduced a corrected calendar in 1582. Naturally, we call it the Gregorian calendar, and it's the one we use today. (You get to name things after yourself if you're pope, too.) The Gregorian calendar is much more accurate. When it was introduced, we went from October 4 to October 15 in one day. They got rid of ten days. That's convenient. I can think of ten days here and there in my life I might like to get rid of.

But in 1531, the Gregorian calendar was 51 years in the future.

By the time Juan Diego met Our Lady on Tepayac Hill, the Julian calendar had got far enough out of whack that December 12 was actually the winter solstice. And on the image of Our Lady of Guadalupe is the constellation of the stars on the night of the winter solstice. It really was *exactly* the middle of winter when Juan Diego picked those flowers. Not just approximately the middle of winter, but exactly.

What is the winter solstice all about? It's the shortest day of the year. It's the darkest time of the year. But it's the time when light starts to come back into the world.

He must increase; I must decrease.

John the Baptist was born on June 24—just after the summer solstice. Six months later, Christ was born—just after the winter solstice.

He must increase.

Now think of the time.

In 1517, Martin Luther had nailed his Ninety-Five Theses to the church door in Wittenberg, beginning the Protestant separation from the Catholic Church. Just at the beginning of 1531, Henry VIII had forced the clergy in England to recognize him as the Supreme Head of the Church of England, setting in motion what would become a complete separation of the English Church from Rome.

Millions of Catholics in Europe had defected from the faith—whether they liked it or not, since Henry soon made it a death-penalty offense to deny that he was head of the Church in England.

It was the darkest time the Church had known in centuries. It was the winter of our discontent, to steal a phrase from Shakespeare.

But at the darkest moment, the winter solstice of the Church, came the ray of light at Guadalupe. Our Lady has always had an eye for symbols, and not only did she appear right at the darkest day of the year, but she also appeared in a way that would show her Mexican children exactly who she was. In the image she left on Juan Diego's cloak, she was dressed as royalty, wearing a mantle of stars, like a Mexican goddess. But instead of looking cruel and bloodthirsty, she looked mild and humble. She was praying, to show that she wasn't a goddess after all—she was there to lead the people to the true God. It was a language of visual symbols that every Mexican could understand.

And they fell in love with her.

Millions fell away in Europe. But suddenly millions more were flocking to the Church in America.

Our Lady appeared, and the pagan and superstitious Aztecs—and that's being charitable, saying it that way—saw a new scene of purity and humility, of hope and goodness. The scales fell from their eyes.

What was not *humanly* possible was supernaturally possible. The friars had no hope of succeeding by themselves. But they didn't have to do it by themselves.

Maybe that was why Columbus' voyage seemed to have so many Marian overtones. Maybe it was because Mary was waiting for someone to come across the sea and prepare the way for her, so she could lead the whole hemisphere to her Son.

Her prediction to St. James was coming true. The Spanish were taking the faith all over the world. And they were only getting started. There was still the rest of Central and South America, and then the Philippines in Asia—where Our Lady of Guadalupe is also revered.

The number of Christians around the world was being multiplied astronomically.

And that was good for the Church. Because back in Europe, Christendom was in trouble.

7. The Battle for Christendom

In 1453, Constantinople fell to the Turks.

That's one of those boring facts of history that make your eyes glaze over. Yeah, there was this battle in this year, and then there was that battle in that year, and then there was another battle in another year, and there's going to be a test on this, isn't there?

Let me tell you why this isn't just another random date.

This was the end of the Roman Empire.

You remember the Roman Empire. The western half of it disappeared in 476. But the eastern half of it, in spite of Arab invasions and Turkish conquests, lasted for another thousand years.

Altogether, since Julius Caesar, the Roman Empire had been going for about 1500 years.

That's a long time.

And for the last 1100 years of that time, it had been a Christian empire.

Now, there wasn't much left of it by 1453. The "Empire" was mostly Constantinople and a little bit of land around it. But Constantinople was the biggest, most important city in the East, and it still had a fleet that kept the Turks distracted.

And keeping the Turks distracted was important, because they were pouring into Europe.

Already they had most of the Balkans. In fact they had completely surrounded Constantinople and the little bit of land that still made up the so-called Roman Empire.

But Constantinople was always the prize. The legendary city with its legendary treasures was the thing the Turkish sultan really wanted. So it was the thing he spent a lot of his energy on.

Now he had it.

In the next century, the remaining Christian possessions in the East fell one by one. The Ottoman Empire, the empire of the sultans, got stronger and stronger. Nothing could defeat them, it seemed. Especially at sea. For most of the next century, the Turkish navy never lost an important battle.

And that brings us up to 1571.

Holy League

The pope at the time was St. Pius V. It had been a while since a pope was a saint. You have to go back two centuries even to find a blessed. But things were changing in Rome, and now there was a saint for a pope. He wouldn't be canonized till later, of course, but it was already pretty obvious that there was something different about this pope.

He wasn't just a saint, though. He was also a smart operator in politics. He managed to do what no pope had done in 300 years: he united a whole group of Catholic Christian countries in one common cause. Spain, Portugal, Venice, Malta, Sicily, Genoa, and of course the Papal States—they were all together in one Holy League. And they had a mission: to get rid of the Turkish navy.

That was a big job. The Turks had been flexing their muscles. In the century since they conquered Constantinople, they were going from conquest to conquest, and they hadn't been afraid to sail right up to the coast of Italy and thumb their noses at everybody. They had just taken Cyprus. What was next? Maybe Venice? Maybe Rome? Who knew? And if they got Italy, Spain would be next on the menu. They'd have a chance to undo the Reconquista. And with Spain would come that vast new empire in America—the place where millions of new souls had just been won for the Church.

Things were looking desperate for Christendom.

And the Turks were not very nice to Christians. In those days ships in the Mediterranean were propelled by oars. Rowing a ship was a nasty job, and Turkish soldiers didn't want to do it. So they used Christian slaves captured in battle instead. That was a thing every Christian knew about the Turkish navy: lose a battle, and you end up rowing their ships.

So you'd better not lose.

The man in charge of the expedition was Don John (or Juan, because he had Spanish relatives, too) of Austria, the illegitimate son of Charles V. Illegitimate—but, hey, he was talented. King Philip of Spain was his half-brother, and Philip was the one who insisted on having John as the leader. You take John, he told Pope Pius, or you don't get Spain. Pope Pius took John. He had no reason to regret the choice.

It was going to be a tough job. The Turkish fleet was much bigger than anything the Holy League could put together. The Turks had all the experience. And the Turks were on a roll, which means a lot in war. Your soldiers don't want to face an enemy who seems unstoppable.

John was a man of sincere faith. He wasn't going in without help. A copy of the miraculous image of Our Lady of Guadalupe, touched to the original, had been sent over from Mexico, and it was on his ship. But even so, John must have had moments when he thought the Holy League didn't have a prayer.

Our Lady of Victory

But prayer was exactly what they did have.

The Holy League's fleet sailed eastward to meet the Turks. And as the fleet sailed, the pope put all of Christendom to work.

He called on every Christian in Europe to pray for victory. And the prayer he chose was the Rosary.

So as the fleet sailed, all of Catholic Europe was praying the Rosary. The pope himself led a Rosary procession in Rome, even though he was so sick at the time that he could hardly walk. Rome's greatest treasure, an icon of the Virgin and Child called the *Salus Populi Romani* (Salvation of the Roman People) was brought out of its home in the church of St. Mary Major and carried with the procession. That was something no one living had seen: the icon is one of the ancient images that tradition says

St. Luke himself painted, and it is only brought out in times of great danger or great joy.

Everywhere, countless Christians prayed. And the victory was won.

On October 7, 1571, the Holy League's fleet met a much larger Turkish fleet, and completely overwhelmed the Turks. Thousands of Christian slaves were freed from the Turkish ships they had been rowing.

In a moment, the world changed.

Pope Pius himself was sitting back in the office doing paperwork with his secretary. But he knew the moment the victory was won. No one could say how, but he knew it. He jumped up and announced that this wasn't a time for filling out forms. It was a time for celebration and thanksgiving.

It was only days later, when the news reached Italy, that the rest of the world knew he wasn't crazy.

And once again, we find Mary at the crossroads of history.

The Pope proclaimed October 7 the feast of Our Lady of Victory. It's also known as the Feast of Our Lady of the Rosary, because the Rosary prayers all over Christendom had made the impossible possible.

I can't tell you what a big change this made in Europe. The best way to say it is that, in one day, all of Europe went from despair to hope. It seemed like Turkish conquest was inevitable. Imagine what it must be like to know it's coming, and there's nothing you can do about it.

And then, suddenly, there *was* something you could do about it. The Turks *could* be defeated.

If you ever go to Barcelona, go to the cathedral there. I'm not talking about Sagrada Familia, the striking Art Nouveau masterpiece by Gaudi. That's the church everybody thinks of when they think of Barcelona, but it's not the cathedral. The Cathedral of the Holy Cross and St. Eulalia is one of those Gothic masterpieces we talked about from the height of the Middle Ages, You could spend hours in it and not see all the masterpieces of art. But one place you should definitely make time for is at the back of the cathedral, on the left. It's the Chapel of Lepanto.

Right at the entrance is a crucifix, and you might not even pay much attention to it if you didn't know where it came from. What's one more crucifix among all those works of art? You might be suffering from art overload by this time.

But this is the crucifix that was on the prow of John of Austria's ship at the Battle of Lepanto. This was the sign that he relied on divine assistance rather than any skill of his own. Not that he didn't have skill, and not that he didn't use it, but John knew where to put his priorities. This crucifix hangs in the cathedral of Barcelona to remind the world that John of Austria put his priorities in the right place.

And there's one more footnote to that battle. One of the many soldiers injured at the battle was a young man named Miguel de Cervantes Saavedra. We don't think of him as a soldier, of course. We think of him as the author of the most famous novel ever written, *Don Quixote.* Would we ever have had the immortal adventures of Don Quixote and Sancho Panza if the Turkish expansion hadn't been stopped?

Of course the Turks weren't destroyed. The Ottoman Empire lasted until 1922, and for a long time it was still a force to be reckoned with. It wasn't about to pull back and give up. And a century later, the Turks were pouring into Europe again.

This time they came by land.

The last battle for Europe

For two months the Turks had been besieging Vienna. It was the furthest they had come into Europe for a century and a half. And if they took Vienna, the rest of Europe might as well just open the gates to them. Vienna controlled the way from everywhere to everywhere else. But could they be stopped? The defenders in Vienna were badly outnumbered.

But there was one thing they had going for them. The Holy Roman Empire, which Austria was part of at the time, had made an alliance with Poland to counter the Turks. And that turned out to be a very smart idea. The King of Poland was John Sobieski, and—like Don John of Austria back in 1571—he knew where to look for help.

The Emperor, who had run away from Vienna when the Turks showed up, called on Sobieski to come help out a bit. Sobieski was marching his troops to relieve Vienna, and they passed the shrine of Our Lady of Czestochowa. There they prayed for Our Lady's intercession and dedicated the whole army to Our Lady. Then, marching as fast as they could manage, the army arrived at Vienna on September 11.

On September 12, 1683, Sobieski's army routed the Turks, who went running all the way out of Austria. The Turkish general lived to report his defeat to the Sultan, and be strangled for his defeat. Turkish performance reviews were tough in those days.

Sobieski used all his knowledge of tactics and all his courage to defeat the Turks. But he didn't take any credit for himself. "I came, I saw, God conquered." That was what he wrote to the pope in announcing his victory.

September 12, as it happened, was celebrated in some places as the feast of the Most Holy Name of Mary. Now, in response to the great victory at Vienna, the pope extended that celebration to the whole Church —a feast that was out of the calendar for a few years, but was reinstated by Pope John Paul II.

And what other date did you think of when you heard the story of the battle? Some see the terrorist attacks on America from September 11 as timed to the anniversary of the arrival of John Sobieski's relief force.

Once again, Mary stands at the crossroads of history.

8. The Century of Fatima

It is very important to trust people. But it is also very important to verify claims. I am grateful that I always trusted my parents, because I know they never told me a lie. I also know that they never told me the whole story when they asked me to pray for a "special intention." The request was simultaneously clear but vague, in order to protect the good name and reputation of others. Still, it's part of my curious nature to look for proofs to support claims. There are a lot of con artists out there, and some like to make a living from the Church.

I also used to work for a CPA group for three years. I did audits. You might be surprised by this, but some people who handle companies' money deceive themselves and in turn deceive others, not always due to malice, but sometimes weakness, and not infrequently incompetence.

Yes, I trust people, but I really trust them when they prove it.

Let's not be naive. If there isn't transparency, if there isn't accountability, you really can't trust the statement, can you?

Enough said. I won't go farther. I only bring it up to explain that I understand why it took the Church so long to really accept the visions at Fatima officially, and at a universal level. And I also understand why the Church finally did accept them. Once you can account for everything in the ledger, you stop doubting. It took fifty years before a pope would visit Fatima: St. Paul VI in 1967. Then St. John Paul II, Benedict XVI, and now Pope Francis have all visited this pivotal shrine.

And there's no question that the apparitions at Fatima are one of the great turning points in history. They're a turning point in the history of the Church. They could be a turning point in the history of the world. The great Archbishop Fulton Sheen thought that Our Lady chose this out-of-the-way little place in Portugal for a reason—a reason that had everything to do with the name. Remember, he said, how much respect Muslims have for Mary. Remember that for them, as for us, she is the most blessed of all women. And remember that the only woman who comes close to that blessedness is Fatima, the daughter of Mohammed.

> Since nothing ever happens out of heaven except with a finesse of all details, I believe that the Blessed Virgin chose to be known as "Our Lady of Fatima" as a pledge and a sign of hope to the Muslim people, and as an assurance that they, who show her so much respect, will one day accept her Divine Son, too.[15]

Three secrets

So it's 1917. You probably know the story of Our Lady of Fatima. Three children in Portugal—Jacinta, Francisco, Lucia—and Our Lady chooses them of all people to make a special request. She gave them three secrets.

The first was that there would be another great war (remember the First World War was going on at the time.)

The second was that the Holy Father needed to consecrate Russia to the Immaculate Heart of Mary. If he doesn't, Russia will spread her errors all throughout the world. The Holy Father will have much to suffer, entire nations will be annihilated, and in the end my Immaculate Heart will triumph.

And the third was a vision of the pope being shot.

Our Lady also predicted that Jacinta and Francisco would die soon. And they did, carried off by the worldwide flu epidemic at the end of the war.

So this is 1917. Why did it take so long for John Paul II to consecrate Russia to the Immaculate Heart of Mary? He didn't do it until four years after he was shot. Why?

Because the American priest who popularized Our Lady of Fatima, Father Walsh, wrote the book in the fifties, and Sister Lucia did not release

---

[15] Fulton J. Sheen, *The World's First Love*, p. 203.

the first two prophecies until 1941. The third was kept a secret in the archives of the Congregation for the Doctrine of the Faith.

Trust, but verify.

Well, wait a second.

The Second World War has already started. Kristallnacht already happened in 1938. Russia's already Communist and atheist—

You can't fool me! You're writing these things after the fact! How do you expect me to believe it?

They've got a lot of smart people in the Vatican. They had to be skeptical. It's their job to be skeptical.

And you can't just say, well, there are lots of people who believe it, so it must be true. Yes, there are millions of people going to Fatima, but you know there are a million people buying bad used cars every day. People are gullible. Especially people who didn't have seven older brothers and sisters like me.

What changed even the most skeptical minds in the Vatican about Fatima was May 13, 1981. The day Mehmet Ali Agca gunned down St. John Paul II in St. Peter's Square. A marble plaque in the pavement marks that spot.

That was the day Pope John Paul II really learned to believe in Fatima.

When John Paul II was elected pope, it seemed like anything could happen. For the first time in more than four centuries, the pope was a cardinal from outside Italy. And not just from outside Italy—he was from the other side of the Iron Curtain. The pope was from Poland—an officially atheist country that was, nevertheless, filled with Catholics.

That had the Communists worried.

And with good reason. The people of Poland erupted with demonstrations of enthusiasm that must have scared the pants off the dictators.

And the next year, the new pope visited his home country and brought the most dangerous message the Communist authorities had ever heard.

He stood up in front of the biggest crowds in the history of Communist Poland and told them, "Do not be afraid."

Do not be afraid? But the whole authority of Communism was built on fear! If people stopped being afraid, how would the dictators keep them in line?

This cardinal from Krakow had suddenly become the single most feared man in the Communist world. At least feared by the dictators.

It wasn't just the dictators who didn't know what to do about him. John Paul spoke fearlessly, telling people things they didn't always want to hear.

But he also brought the Gospel to people who had never paid attention to it before. He was the poster pope for evangelization, the one who traveled more than any other pope before him, maybe more than all the others put together.

But what made him such a powerhouse? Where did he get his courage?

You can learn practically everything you need to know about John Paul from his coat of arms.

The Marian Cross

In the Middle Ages, the art of heraldry was developed into a science. The "coat of arms" that a nobleman carried was supposed to tell you at a glance what was most important to know about him. People of the Middle Ages could read coats of arms the same way we read traffic signs. A squiggly arrow pointing up? Oh, that means there's a series of curves ahead. The symbols in heraldry convey information just as quickly to someone who knows how to read them.

Every prince has a coat of arms, of course. And a bishop is a prince.

So what do you see in John Paul's coat of arms? Of course there are the triple crown and keys that every pope has in his arms—those show that he's pope, the successor of St. Peter, who was given the keys of the kingdom by Christ. But in the shield is where you see what's unique to John Paul.

And what's in the shield is just an off-center cross with the letter M in the lower right corner.

That's the Marian Cross. The M is for Mary. She's in the lower right because she stands at the foot of the cross.

Would you be surprised to learn that John Paul wore the brown scapular of the Carmelites? One look at his coat of arms, and you know: here's a man who's devoted to Mary—and through Mary, above all, to Christ.

And with that devotion he could face anything.

Which brings us to May 13, 1981.

The third secret

On that day the pope was riding into St. Peter's Square as usual. And as usual, crowds of people were there to see him.

Suddenly a man who had been sitting on the edge of the crowd stood up and started shooting.

Four bullets hit the pope. Two of them stayed in his intestines.

That was May 13. It was the feast of Our Lady of Fatima.

The man who shot him was an expert. He should have killed his target. But as John Paul II in the hospital said, "One hand pulled the trigger, another guided the bullet." He had always relied on the Blessed Mother's protection. He had been wearing that brown scapular when he was shot. Now he knew for certain that he hadn't relied on her in vain.

So he made a decision. "Bring me that third secret of Fatima in the Congregation for the Doctrine of the Faith."

That's when he became a believer in Fatima. It was forced on him by an assassin's bullet.

John Paul was not naive. He knew God acted in history. He didn't just take things at face value. But now he had a bullet in his gut. And the Soviet army was waiting with their tanks on the border of Poland. And Cardinal Stefan Wyszyński, the greatest figure in the Polish resistance to Communism, was on his deathbed in Poland. And Ronald Reagan was still recovering from his own attempted assassination in the United States. It was the height of the Cold War.

The year 1981 was also the peak of abortion in our country, the peak of divorce in our country, it's the peak of the sexual abuse by priests in our country.

And it was the year Our Lady appeared at Medjugorje. It was the year she started to appear at Kibeho to warn about the coming Rwandan genocide. This was a pivotal year.

History could tip one way or the other. It was an inflection point.

But Our Lady stepped in.

John Paul still had his greatest work to do, and she had to preserve him for that. A few years later, St. John Paul II consecrated Russia to the Immaculate Heart of Mary in unison with all of the Bishops of the world. Soon a man named Mikhail S. Gorbachev would lead the USSR and speak about "Glasnost." People wondered if this "Michael" might have been secretly baptized by his grandmother when he was a child, and might be an answer to all the prayers to St. Michael after Mass for the conversion of Russia.

I vividly remember the day Gorbachev came to Rome to visit John Paul II. December 1, 1989, less than one month after the gates of freedom were opened on the Berlin Wall (November 9, 1989) and crowds swarmed on top of the wall in jubilation for being free at last. I ditched class in Rome the day Gorbachev came to visit the Roman Pontiff! All the TV and Radio stations and newspapers from around the world were there to witness that historic event, something that might happen once in a thousand years, like Henry IV finally offering obedience to the great medieval Pope Gregory VII (Hildebrandus) at Canossa. The next day the New York Times reported:

> With an agreement to begin official relations and a pledge of expanded religious freedom for Soviet citizens, President Mikhail S. Gorbachev joined hands today with Pope John Paul II.
>
> Seven decades of spiritual and philosophical conflict came to a symbolic end as the two talked for more than an hour in the

heart of Vatican City, the first encounter between a Soviet Communist leader and a Pope.

The Communist leaders feared Karol Wojtyla because he spoke truth and he did not fear them. Ultimately, they could not survive this Polish Pope, the man who came from a far country, who rallied the faithful from the moment of his election echoing the words of Jesus: "Do not be afraid!"

The Iron Curtain came crashing down in 1991. Not long after, in 1992, a few of the old-timers tried to take over in what was left of the Soviet Union and bring it back to orthodox Communism. But it was too late. The people of Russia had seen that anything was possible. They'd seen that they didn't have to be afraid. And the Soviet Union came crashing down, too.

Meanwhile, John Paul himself had some unfinished business with Our Lady at Fatima.

The hand that guided the bullet

The year after he was shot, the pope went to Fatima. He brought that nine-millimeter bullet with him that the surgeons had removed from his gut, and he placed it in the crown of Our Lady of Fatima.

Then what happens? Now the Vatican's talking about canonizing those two children, Jacinta and Francisco. Maybe they *weren't* making it up.

There's a lot of pushback. Some of the cardinals are saying, "Now, look, you can't canonize children. They weren't martyrs. They can't possibly live virtue heroically."

But the people who argued for the canonizations said, yes, they can. They prayed. They did penance. They died early as it was predicted. Lucia went to the monastery. They were walking the walk of the followers of Christ.

And that was the argument that won the day. For the first time in the whole history of the Catholic Church, children who were not martyred were canonized.

Think what that means.

Your children can be saints. Your grandchildren can be saints.

And that's a good reason, if we needed a good reason, for every Catholic to join the battle on the side of life.

9. The Battle for Life— and Relevant Radio's Part in It

Remember how we began at the end of 1999?

Now, a lot of people thought of that as the last day of the millennium. But it really wasn't. (In spite of what I told those kids on the way through Nebraska. But give me a break! I was desperate.) We still had another year to go.

That's because there isn't a year 0. We start counting at 1. And a millennium is a thousand years. So count from one to a thousand, and the last number is 1000. You don't start another thousand till you get to 1001. Then you count another thousand, and you're not finished till you hit 2000.

So the new millennium really began on January 1, 2001, because there aren't any 999-year millennia in our calendar.

And I mention that because it was right as we were changing millennia, for real this time, that there was another important change in history. How important? Too early to tell.

To be specific, it was December 12, 2000.

What happened then?

The United States Supreme Court declared that the election of George Bush was valid. It all came down to Florida. Remember that? The "hanging chads"? The vote was so close that they kept recounting it.

But what else is December 12? You probably remember: it's the feast of Our Lady of Guadalupe. It's the commemoration of the time Our Lady came to Juan Diego, at a place that's now part of the giant metropolis of Mexico City.

Our Lady of Guadalupe, Star of the New Evangelization. Our Lady of Guadalupe, Patroness of the unborn, Patroness of the Americas.

What's the first thing the new president did? He reinstated the Mexico City Policy. It was a policy that was first announced at a UN conference in Mexico City during the Reagan administration, which is why the name "Mexico City" has stuck to it ever since. It had been rescinded by the Clinton administration, but George W. Bush made it his first priority to put it back in place.

"It is my conviction that taxpayer funds should not be used to pay for abortions or advocate or actively promote abortion, either here or abroad," he said, reinstating the policy by executive order.

And Bush was put in office by a Supreme Court decision handed down on the feast of Our Lady of Guadalupe, patroness of Mexico, patroness of the unborn, whose shrine is in Mexico City. Coincidence? Or Mary at the crossroads of history?

It's still too early to tell how big an event that was. The policy was rescinded again by the next Democrat in the White House, and reinstated by the Republican after that. We have a long way to go before we conquer the evil of abortion. But how many lives did it save? How many thousands of children didn't die because the U.S. wouldn't fund abortions overseas?

Now, going back to December 12, 2000, there's one other big important event that happened on that day. It's an event of such colossal proportions that people who lived through it will remember it to the day they die, and their grandchildren will still be talking about it, and their grandchildren's grandchildren will pass it down to their grandchildren.

On December 12, 2000, the Federal Communications Commission in Washington, D.C., granted Relevant Radio its first license to broadcast.

All right, so maybe I'm being a *little* self-serving here. But it certainly was a big deal to *me*. And I do think that Relevant Radio makes a big difference in our country. It reaches a majority of the population now. Most people in the country have the opportunity to hear it if they want to. Instead of the dull pop music and vulgar talk shows the other stations carry, they can actually hear something that will improve their spiritual lives, give them hope and save their souls.

And we got our license on December 12, 2000—the last Feast of Our Lady of Guadalupe of the last millennium.

That's why, whenever you see information from Relevant Radio, you will see that icon of Our Lady of Guadalupe.

The Luminous Mysteries

When the new millennium began, John Paul II was still pope. John Paul lived a long time, and in the last years he was very ill. But he kept going. He had spent most of his life teaching us how to live, and now he was teaching us how to die.

And in the very last year of his life, 2005, he had another great gift for us. He added the Luminous Mysteries to the Rosary. That was his swan song.

I know it shocked a lot of Catholics when he did that. People said, "Can he *do* that? Isn't that like adding a fourth person of the Holy Trinity?" It was a change, and sometimes we're afraid of change.

But, no, it's not a fourth person of the Holy Trinity. The Rosary, like other practices in the Church, evolves over time. The truth doesn't change, but we adapt the way we respond to it. And this is a beautiful addition to the prayer Christians have been praying since St. Dominic.

These are the Luminous Mysteries:

1. The baptism in the Jordan.
2. The wedding at Cana.
3. The proclamation of the Kingdom in Galilee.
4. The Transfiguration.

And the best one:

5. The institution of the Holy Eucharist.

And that was John Paul's final year: the Year of the Eucharist.

What a gift to leave behind!

And now we're going to bring our story all the way home to America. The Midwest, even. It's December 8, 2010, and that's the next big day in history as far as I'm concerned.

Does that date sound familiar to you?

That was the day the Bishop of Green Bay, David Ricken, formally approved an apparition of the Blessed Mother that had taken place on October 8, 1859, to a young immigrant woman from Belgium known as Adele Brice.

The apparition of Our Lady of Good Help took place just twenty miles from Green Bay. It was a big deal when this was approved.

And some people rolled their eyes.

There was only one news service or media service that covered it live that day: Relevant Radio.

ABC was not there. CNN was not there. The New York Times missed it completely.

Why do I say it was a big deal, then?

Because there have only been 16 times in modern history since 1531 to today that a supposed apparition has been approved. Fatima and Guadalupe and Lourdes are the most well known, of course. But this is our apparition for this country.

And I'll bet you haven't heard of it. Unless you listen a lot to Relevant Radio.

Our Lady in Wisconsin

When I started at Relevant Radio in 2009, one of the ladies in the office said, "Father Rocky, did you hear Our Lady appeared out in the woods by Green Bay?"

Well, I hear a lot of things. And I know from experience that the vast majority of reputed apparitions are never accepted by the Church as being of supernatural origin. In fact, when dealing with claims of the supernatural, there can be hysteria and superstition, leading people away from their normal jobs and responsibilities that they should be focusing on. That's why I am, by nature, very cautious to promote an "apparition" until it has been officially approved by the Church.

So I was careful and guarded in my response when the good people in Green Bay told me about this apparition I had never heard about.

Nine months went by. One day in May of 2009 we drove out to the little shrine of Our Lady of Good Help by Green Bay. We walked in and saw the tabernacle in the center, covered with a veil, but sparkling because of the lighting, and an angel on either side kneeling in wonderful adoration. The simple linoleum tiles on the floor were dazzlingly clean. Here and there people were sitting quietly and reverently in the pews. And I just had a sense that there was something *real* here. There was an extraordinary and overwhelming sense of peace and authentic reverence in this holy place. It was just an impression, but I don't ignore those impressions. Sometimes they lead me somewhere worth going.

Then I had to find out what the story was.

Here's the story. There was a little girl in Belgium. When she was in the second grade, she and her friends said, "When we grow up, we want to be teaching sisters like our nuns." They all decided that at the same time.

But this girl Adele had a rough time, and it looked as though she would never get to live the life she had planned for herself.

In eighth grade she had to quit school to work on the farm. Two years later she had a terrible accident with lye soap, and it left her disfigured and blind.

She was 23 years old when her parents decided they were going to move to America. Since Adele didn't have a way of taking care of herself, and since they thought she didn't have much chance of attracting a husband, they told her she was going with them.

She didn't want to go. She wanted to stay in Belgium and become a nun.

But she did the right thing. She went to the priest and asked his advice.

He said, "Adele, you really ought to go with your parents. If God wants you to be a nun in America, you'll be a nun in America."

So they went up towards the Green Bay area. In those days—this was back in 1855—there were lots of people who were eager to sell cheap real estate way out west to poor immigrants. And in those days, believe it or not, real-estate salesmen weren't always honest. I know it's a shock, but it's true.

Adele and her family got to the land outside Green Bay. And it turned out to be not quite what it was cracked up to be. It was a lot of hard work. The land was not all that good. They had to clear thick forest. They were working around the clock and hardly surviving.

One day Adele was walking through the woods, and in the woods she saw an image of a beautiful woman. Blonde hair, white dress, yellow sash. She was sure, somehow, that this was something supernatural. Maybe it had something to do with the way the woman was surrounded by a blaze of light and had a crown of stars over her head.

No words were exchanged.

The vision disappeared.

A week later Adele was walking through the woods again, this time with her mother and her sister. And again she saw that same radiant woman, with blonde hair—blonde hair!—yellow sash, white gown.

No words were exchanged. And when she asked her mother and her sister about it, it turned out they hadn't seen anything.

So Adele walked fifteen miles to the closest Catholic church, talked to the priest, and reported what she saw.

The priest said, "Adele, if this happens again, this is what you are to say: 'In God's name, who are you, and what do you want?'"

A week later, after returning from Mass, she saw the same vision in the woods. She remembered what the priest had told her. So she spoke to the vision: "In God's name, who are you, and what do you want?"

And Our Lady responded, "I am the Queen of Heaven."

This was October 9, 1859. One year earlier, Our Lady had appeared at Lourdes, where she said, "I am the Immaculate Conception."

The Immaculate Conception is the beginning of her existence. And her ultimate destination was Queen of Heaven.

"I am the Queen of Heaven who prays for the conversion of sinners," Our Lady told Adele. "And I want you to do the same. Gather the children in this wild country and teach them what they need to know for their salvation. Teach them to make the sign of the cross. Teach them to approach the sacraments fruitfully. Teach them their catechism. You went to Mass, received Communion. You've done well. You need to do more. You need to pray, you need to do penance, you need to make a confession. Go, and I will help you."

That was it.

Note how specific and simple Our Lady's instructions were. Teach them to make the sign of the cross. Pope Francis has picked up on this, by the way. He's telling parents and grandparents, teach your kids and grandkids to make the sign of the cross. This is the Catholic 101 thing that we do. And we do it because, simple as it is, it's a constant reminder of our faith. It's a constant reminder that we're Christians, and Jesus died on the cross for us.

Teach them their catechism. Teach them what they need to know for their salvation.

And, of course, before you start your work, make a general confession.

It all sounded so simple and easy. And it was what Adele had always wanted to do with her life.

So she went home and told her parents, "Mom, Dad, I need to stop working on the farm and teach the kids their catechism."

Her parents weren't as enthusiastic about that idea as she might have hoped.

"You can't do that! We need you on the farm. We're barely getting by as it is."

"Well," she suggested, "what if I work really fast and get my chores done early?"

"Well..." They thought about that for a moment. "Well, then you can do it."

They probably thought it was a safe thing to say. There was so much work to do on the farm that it seemed impossible that Adele could get done early. But if she did—well, the work would be done.

So Adele worked hard and got her chores done early. Then she went down the road to the next farm and said, "Could I teach your kids their catechism? They're not learning their faith."

And she ran into exactly the same problem.

The farmer there said, "We need them to work on the farm. They can't take time off for catechism classes."

But by now Adele had figured out the solution to that problem. "Well, how about if I help them work on their chores and we finish early?"

"Well..." And again the same calculation. How could it hurt to have an extra hand around the farm? Especially one who worked for free? "Well, yeah, then you could do it."

And so it went, with Adele going from one farm to another, doing chores and teaching the catechism.

In no time, the farmers were saying, "You know, Adele's doing a good thing here, gathering the children and teaching them the faith. I don't know whether we believe in this crazy apparition of hers, but let's build her a little brick schoolhouse for the kids."

After a short time, they weren't doubting the apparition so much anymore. Adele's father built a little wooden chapel, and then the people of the area built a larger chapel that could hold quite a few people. Over the door was written (in French), "Our Lady of Good Help, Pray for Us."

Now here's the part of the story where I really got convinced.

Exactly twelve years after the apparition, on October 8 and 9, 1871, there was a great fire.

Saved from the inferno

Everybody remembers the story of the Great Chicago Fire. The weather had been hot and intensely dry for a long time. There had been *one inch* of rain in the past three months. And then the wind picked up —a hot, dry wind.

A little fire started in Mrs. O'Leary's barn—it was blamed on her cow kicking over a lamp, because the cow wasn't going to contradict anyone.

When it was over, the city was devastated, three hundred people had died, and a hundred thousand were homeless.

Everybody remembers that story.

What everyone has forgotten was that, that same day, northern Wisconsin burned down. I'm not exaggerating much. I'll tell you a little about it here, but when you get a chance, look up that historical event: the Peshtigo Fire. You'll discover that whatever I say here doesn't do it justice.

Peshtigo is a little town in northern Wisconsin. That's where the fire started. The whole northern part of Wisconsin was as dry as Chicago. Little fires were already burning here and there when the wind came.

And suddenly it was hell on earth.

The wind whipped up the little fires into a gigantic firestorm that obliterated everything in its path. No one knows how many people were killed, because everything was incinerated beyond recognition. The lowest possible number is about 1200, which is four times the number that died in the Great Chicago Fire at the same time. It might have been twice that many, or even more. The few who survived saw sights that must have haunted their nightmares for the rest of their lives. Some terrified witnesses watched as the fire formed itself into a tornado that threw flaming houses and train cars around like toys.

And Adele Brise, now a nun, was right in the path of the inferno.

Fortunately, she knew what to do. She relied on Our Lady of Good Help.

She led everybody she could find into the chapel where Our Lady had appeared to her.

All around them the flames swirled. The fire was everywhere outside.

But anybody who ran to the little chapel where Our Lady appeared— all of them were saved.

And they wrote about it.

Adele grabbed the statue of Our Lady and said, "Let's go outside and pray the Rosary."

She prayed the Rosary along the western perimeter, and the fire moved with the wind to the north. She went to the northern perimeter, it moved up there. All night long they were doing this Rosary procession, carrying this image of Our Lady.

The next day, it rained. The fire was extinguished.

They looked out: north, south, east, west, as far as you could see, everything was obliterated.

But not the chapel.

This is historical record. The people who were there were saved. They called on Our Lady of Good Help, and she did the impossible.

This was the story that had been passed down for generations in that part of Wisconsin, and well documented by contemporary records. But it was always a local devotion. No one had ever officially investigated it.

So in 2008, when Bishop David Ricken was appointed the new bishop there, the previous bishop told him about it. Bishop Zubik was going to Pittsburgh—he'd only been in Green Bay for four years. It wasn't enough time for him to do an investigation, but it was enough time for him to get interested. So he told his successor, "You know, you need to investigate what's going on there. It's been going on for 150 years. You need to get some theologians to look into it."

Bishop Ricken did just that. And after two years, he came to the conclusion that the events, locutions, and words that happened here in October of 1859 "are of supernatural origin" and therefore worthy to be believed. Although not obligatory, of course, which is the way the Church always approves these apparitions.

Now the United States has its own officially approved Marian apparition. The. Only. One.

And I, for one, am going to make a lot of use of Our Lady of Good Help. Because I think we need all the help we can get.

10. What We Can Do—With Our Lady's Help

Look back again at that vision in the middle of the book of Revelation. It's in Revelation 12, starting at the beginning.

> A great sign appeared in the sky, a woman clothed with the sun, with the moon under her feet, and on her head a crown of twelve stars. She was with child and wailed aloud in pain as she labored to give birth.

This vision that reminds us so much of Mary as Our Lady of Guadalupe is also, as we said before, a vision of the Church giving birth to us. But what happens next?

> Then another sign appeared in the sky; it was a huge red dragon, with seven heads and ten horns, and on its heads were seven diadems. Its tail swept away a third of the stars in the sky and hurled them down to the earth. Then the dragon stood before the woman about to give birth, to devour her child when she gave birth.

Why is the dragon trying to devour the child? It's because of who the dragon is, and who the child is.

> She gave birth to a son, a male child, destined to rule all the nations with an iron rod. Her child was caught up to God and his throne. The woman herself fled into the desert where she had a place prepared by God, that there she might be taken care of for twelve hundred and sixty days.

God doesn't leave his Church, our mother, to fend for herself. The child is saved from the dragon, and the mother is taken care of. And this doesn't make the dragon happy at all.

> Then war broke out in heaven; Michael and his angels battled against the dragon. The dragon and its angels fought back, but they did not prevail and there was no longer any place for them in heaven.

But who is this dragon? Of course you *probably* already know. But St. John doesn't leave it to chance. Most of the book is full of visions dense with symbols that you have to work out for yourself, but here St. John decides it's important to be explicit.

> The huge dragon, the ancient serpent, who is called the Devil and Satan, who deceived the whole world, was thrown down to earth, and its angels were thrown down with it.

This dragon is Satan. And it's the ancient serpent, the same serpent who tempted Adam and Eve in the garden, the same serpent who deceived the whole earth. He's been our enemy from the beginning of history. And he'll be our enemy until the end of history.

The dragon is always at war with the child.

And I think that's exactly what we see today.

Satan is always at war with the child. He's at war with human children, because children are the future of humanity. And humanity is exactly what Satan can never forgive God for.

The child represents hope. Hope for the idea that we *can* have a future. Hope for the idea that we *should* have a future.

Our Lady of Good Help

You remember how no one showed up from the mass media to cover the event when the apparition of Our Lady of Good Help was approved. No one but Relevant Radio. And in those days, Relevant Radio covering it meant, basically, me and Drew Mariani and a small technical crew made up of Marty Jury, Josh Raymond and Damien Schmitt.

If you ask me why I think we have a future, I can tell you very simply. It's because of what I experienced that day outside Green Bay. That, and all the other times I've seen Our Lady step into history. It's because I know that Mary stands at the crossroads of history, waiting for us to ask for her help.

So let me tell you what happened, and how it hanged my life.

We were broadcasting live on Relevant Radio that day when I saw a fellow there I had met in Green Bay some weeks earlier. His name was Michael Lee.

Well, that was an interesting coincidence. I walked over to him and said, "Michael! What are you doing here?"

"Oh, didn't you know?" he answered. "This is where my brother Tommy was cured."

This sounded like the beginning of an interesting story, so I said, "How old's your brother Tommy?"

"Oh, he's probably seventy now."

"When was he cured?" I asked.

"When he was eight years old."

Now I *had* to hear about it. "Well, what's the story?"

"When Tommy was eight, he had these terrible headaches. It was so bad that my parents brought him to the hospital. They gave him an X-ray, and the doctor said, 'He's got this big tumor growing in his head.' And they couldn't do anything about it. So my dad would come out here on the first Friday of every month, take my little brother Tommy, put him on his shoulder, and they'd walk the perimeter of the property, praying the rosary. They did that eight months in a row. They went back to the hospital, they had an X-ray, and the tumor was gone."

"That's an amazing story!" I said when he had finished. "Who knows that?"

"Well, everyone in my family knows it."

"And where is Tommy now?"

"He's down in Arizona. He's married. He's got kids, he's got grand-kids."

"Who else have you told?"

He thought for a moment. "Well, I just told you."

Now I knew I'd made the right choice to come out here. "We've got to tell this to other people! This is an amazing story!"

And soon there were millions of people hearing the story of how Our Lady of Good Help had cured eight-year-old Tommy's brain tumor.

And of course that story got stuck in my mind. It made me start think-ing about what Our Lady of Good Help could help us accomplish.

Walking to Mary

A while later Relevant Radio started promoting the Walk to Mary, ev-ery year on the first Saturday of May, from the National Shrine of St. Joseph at St. Norbert's College in De Pere, Wisconsin, out to the Shrine of Our Lady of Good Help.

Now, this sounds like the sort of thing that might bring in five or six slightly crazy super fans of Our Lady, and maybe a couple of fitness ob-sessives. It's a long hike. It's 21 miles. How many people want to walk 21 miles in a day? A young marine told me, "Wow, Father, that's a really, re-ally long hike!" So how many?

The answer is 2,100 people of all ages who listen to Relevant Radio.

Now, I want to repeat that figure. Twenty-one miles. That's more than marines walk.

And, yes, I'm usually there. I'm not as young as I used to be. But I sup-pose I'm not as old as I will be, so I might as well get my walking in while I can.

This walk has turned into a big thing, the kind of thing that takes a lot of planning, with first-aid stations, portable toilets, all the things you need when you have a couple of thousand people doing a whole lot more physical activity than they're used to.

But, let me tell you, it's worth it.

People come to walk and go away changed. The Walk to Mary is a full body-and-soul experience, and I think it's a great way to deepen your relationship with Jesus, Mary, and Joseph. The way I see it, there are two chief obstacles to living our faith today: the easy life and isolation.

We expect everything to come to us, and we just sit and wait for it to happen. We order food on our smartphones. We never have to go out of the house!

And because we sit in one place, we never meet people. Even when we do go out, we keep our head down, staring into our phone screens, hoping no one will notice us. It would be just *awful* if someone actually talked to us!

But think about what Jesus taught us. Can we live the Christian life in isolation that way?

And I know there were holy hermits who lived in isolation. But that brings us back to the first point. Were they living the easy life? I don't think so.

And that brings us back to the Walk to Mary.

It's not easy to walk twenty-one miles. You're not letting the easy life take over if you do that. It certainly counts as getting out of the house. And you never walk alone. You've got 2,099 friends with you. (I don't promise that will be the exact number.) And they *will* talk to you. If no one else does, I will!

All right, here comes the story you knew was coming. Last year, after the walk, I saw this young lady pushing a baby buggy. And I thought, *I wonder if this is her. I think I met her parents today.*

I had been talking to this couple who told me about how their daughter had five miscarriages in a row. And so she came and did the Walk to Mary the year before, praying for a baby. And she did have a baby.

And, yes, it was the baby in the baby carriage.

I said, "That's you?"

She started weeping.

"Did Our Lady do this for you?"

"Yeah." And then she said, "She's in charge of history."

I don't know why she said that. I don't know what inspired her.

But there she is. Mary at the crossroads of history. Not just world history. Not just our nation's history. Your history, and my history.

All right, well, this was a great story. But it was more than that. It was an inspiration to me personally. I started to remember Our Lady of Good Help when I needed a little bit of help myself.

Well, a couple of years ago, we got a big merger done with Immaculate Heart Radio. We went from reaching sixty million people to reaching one hundred twenty million people. And then more stations came in.

So I said, *Well, now that we're Coast to Coast, let's see what this baby can do!*

You know how it is. If you get a V8 440, you say, "Let's open it up. Let's see what you can do."

Suddenly we had a lot of reach. We'd gone from a Chevette to a Camaro. So I started thinking of how we could change the world. Not that I'm ambitious or anything. But what good is all that power if you never use it?

So how 'bout if we pray the Memorare every hour on air for an end to abortion? Let's see what that will do! Let's just rub it in the face of Satan! Let's just crush his ugly head! Let's see what we can do! Take a page from Mother Teresa's playbook. Let's see what that will do. Let's get kids praying the Memorare on the air. Let's get *bishops* praying the Memorare on the air. Let's see what that will do. So we started praying the Memorare every hour, with no shame, and lots of faith. With thirty thousand people listening and praying at any one moment on our network, the prayers began to add up, like water behind a dam.

In two weeks, Justice Kennedy retired.

Coincidence?

That set up the battle with Kavanaugh. You remember how vicious that was. But the main problem for his opponents was pretty simple.

They were afraid that he was going to vote in favor of life. That's the dividing line in contemporary American politics: the right to life.

And Kavanaugh was confirmed.

Coincidence?

And then legislatures around this country started passing heartbeat laws—laws that either made abortion illegal as soon as a heartbeat could be detected, or, at the very least, mandated that a woman considering an abortion should have to hear the heartbeat of the fetus first to remind her that this was a separate life being ended.

These all started happening after we started our Memorare campaign.

Coincidence? You tell me.

And now, just as I was finishing up this book, President Trump actually spoke at the March for Life. This march has been going on year after year, almost half a century now, bringing in tens of thousands of people in some really appalling January weather. But no president has ever made an appearance at the march—until now.

Coincidence?

"It is my profound honor to be the first president in history to attend the March for Life," the president said. "We are here for a very simple reason: to defend the right of every child, born and unborn, to fulfill their God-given potential." He continued:

> For 47 years, Americans of all backgrounds have traveled from across the country to stand for life.
>
> And today as President of the United States, I am truly proud to stand with you....
>
> We cannot know what our citizens yet unborn will achieve. The dreams they will imagine. The masterpieces they will create. The discoveries they will make. But we know this: every life brings love into this world. Every child brings joy to a family. Every person is worth protecting.

And above all, we know that every human soul is divine and every human life, born and unborn, is made in the holy image of Almighty God.

This wouldn't have happened just a few years ago. Even Republican presidents who *said* they were against abortion never dared to show up at the March for Life.

But we've been praying. And now look what's happening. That may have been the greatest speech ever delivered by an American President, given the consequences of what hangs in the balance.

Your history and mine

We're active players in history, you and I. History isn't just a thing that happens to us. And the Blessed Mother, the Mother of Jesus Christ, is involved in history more than most people are aware, because she is the Mother of God and our Mother, the doorway of history into eternity.

She's willing to give us the help we need. But whatever needs to happen, it's up to you and me to be willing to make the sacrifices to *make* it happen. Our Lady will help with her prayers, and those are more powerful than we can imagine. But we are Christ's body on earth. We're the ones who have to do the work.

That's what's at stake.

We're living in real history. This is the time that God has given us. We can't choose our times. These are the times that come to us. You have to do your part. And I have to do my part.

I am reminded of that pivotal scene in the epic *Lord of the Rings:*

> *Frodo:* I wish the Ring had never come to me. I wish none of this had happened.
> *Gandalf:* So do all who live to see such times, but that is not for them to decide. All we have to decide is what to do with the time that is given to us.

And so we will continue to pray that Memorare on air. And if we get a less than sympathetic administration in Washington, D.C. one day, that wants to suppress our First Amendment rights, *we will stand up.* That was what Saint John Paul the Great said when he came to Washington in 1979. I will never forget his words on October 7, 1979, the Feast of Our Lady of Victory, the Feast of Our Lady of the Rosary. Standing near the altar grasping his iconic silver crozier in his right hand, and with his silver hair tossed by the wind, looking like Gandalf the White, with the United States Capitol in the background as a silhouette for freedom, he pronounced these courageous words for the entire world to hear like a prophet from the Old Testament:

> I do not hesitate to proclaim before you and before the world that all human life—from the moment of conception and through all subsequent stages—is sacred, because human life is created in the image and likeness of God.
>
> And so, we will stand up every time that human life is threatened. When the sacredness of life before birth is attacked, we will stand up and proclaim that no one ever has the authority to destroy unborn life.[16]

I got goosebumps when I heard him speak those words. I instantly recognized his courage in that context, and felt deeply inspired and thanked God for his leadership. Finally. When I heard that, I said to myself, "Holy smokes, that guy's courageous. Somebody's going to shoot him."

I was more prophetic than I'd hoped, I guess. But you don't have to be a prophet to know how the world works. That's what they do to courageous people—they shoot 'em.

---

[16] Holy Mass at the Capital Mall, Homily of His Holiness John Paul II, Washington, Sunday, 7 October 1979 (at http://www.vatican.va/content/john-paul-ii/en/homilies/1979/documents/hf_jp-ii_hom_19791007_usa-washington.html),

But Our Lady intervened that day, didn't she? On May 13, 1981, in St. Peter's square, Mary was there.

And she will be there again and again. I look around me and see more devotion to Mary than ever before.

As I write this, our pope is Francis I. In his first year as pope, he did two remarkable things. Maybe you don't remember them, but I do.

The first was that he dedicated his papacy to Our Lady of Fatima. Exactly two months after he was elected, he had his pontificate solemnly devoted to Our Lady of Fatima by Cardinal Polycarp of Lisbon.

The second was his vigil for peace in Syria and throughout the world later that year. Francis called on all people of good will—Catholic, Protestant, Muslim, Buddhist, even atheist—to join in a vigil for peace. And to underline the importance of the occasion, he brought out the Salus Populi Romani. You remember it: the icon that tradition says Luke painted, which is brought out only for grave emergencies or great celebrations. It came out before the Battle of Lepanto. It came out for Pope Francis' vigil for peace.

Is peace even possible? We still don't have it. And yet Francis wouldn't let us give up on the prospect. To the thousands of people gathered with him in Rome, and to the countless millions paying attention all around the world, Francis gave a message of hope—but also a message of responsibility.

> And at this point I ask myself: Is it possible to walk the path of peace? Can we get out of this spiral of sorrow and death? Can we learn once again to walk and live in the ways of peace? Invoking the help of God, under the maternal gaze of the Salus Populi Romani, Queen of Peace, I say: Yes, it is possible for everyone! From every corner of the world tonight, I would like to hear us cry out: Yes, it is possible for everyone! Or even better, I would like for each one of us, from the least to the greatest, in-

cluding those called to govern nations, to respond: Yes, we want it![17]

The world we live in is broken by sin. But Pope Francis won't give up because he knows that Mary stands at the crossroads of history.

Our history as a world. Our history as a nation. But also your history and my history.

You have your own story about Our Lady in your life—how she intercedes, and the guardian angels. I know you could tell me some amazing stories. You could tell me how she's there with you in your family, in your parish, in your community.

And so I look at the world around us, and I'm filled with hope.

We're living at a difficult moment. I'm not naive. I know how much work there is to do. And I know how dangerous the world is.

But these are our moments! These are the best times to live! This is the best moment to be in! Here we are at the crossroads of history, and Our Lady is here with us, waiting to help us change *everything*. With her help, we can do it. We can make this truly one nation with liberty and justice for *all*—even the most helpless.

That's the drama that we're involved in.

So I'm going to leave you with one more story about Our Lady of Good Help. This is a great story.

A million bucks

I'll spare you the details, but we were completely upside-down at Relevant Radio in 2010, and over our head in debt. The ironic thing was the only way out of debt was to plunge deeper in debt!! We had to buy a station which was worth twice the asking price—but the asking price was way more than we had. We had to cobble together all sorts of investments

---

[17] Vigil of Prayer for Peace, Words of Holy Father Francis, Saint Peter's Square, Saturday, 7 September 2013. On line at http://www.vatican.va/content/francesco/en/homilies/2013/documents/papa-francesco_20130907_veglia-pace.html

and all sorts of donations. We needed one more million dollars, or other-wise we were going to *lose* eight million dollars.

But it just wasn't coming.

This was February of 2011, and by this time I knew where to turn if I needed a little extra help.

So we drove out to the shrine of Our Lady of Good Help. There was snow all around the place. And as we drove in, there was nobody there.

The place looked deserted.

And I said, "You know, only sixteen apparitions of the Blessed Mother have been approved in modern history. And this has got to be the most humble, and therefore it's the strongest. So let's go pray the Rosary, be-cause we need a million bucks."

That's how you've got to pray. Be specific. Million bucks, cash. That's what we need.

So we prayed the Rosary. And then I drove back to Green Bay and walked in my office just as the phone rang.

I picked up the phone. It was a guy I knew who'd been a big help in the past.

"Father, we're going to send you the million dollars."

I was stunned. "That's an answer to prayers! God bless you!!"

In my enthusiasm I kept babbling. "God love you," I said. "I'd give you a kiss on both cheeks, but I won't 'cause you're not Italian and neither am I."

But then I remembered the man I was talking to, and I told him, "I knew you were going to come through for us."

He said, "How'd you know?"

"Because you've got a fifteen-foot statue of the Blessed Mother in your back yard. It's a dead giveaway."

That's Our Lady of Good Help—Mary at the crossroads of history, my own history, giving history a little shove.

Mary is Queen of Angels and Queen of Saints. Mary is Queen of Heaven.

But don't think that puts her far away from us.

We tend to think of heaven as a place that's really really really far away. It's not.

And today, in our world, I think the most important thing is not the Gospel of Mark, not the Gospel of Luke, not the Gospel of Matthew, not the Gospel of John.

It's the Gospel According to You.

Why do *you* believe Jesus Christ is God?

Those prayers that he's answered—write them down on a piece of paper, never forget them. Big things and small things. Keep that journal. The list will grow. Bring it out from time to time to read it and remember, ponder and rejoice. You will be responding to what St. Peter told the early Christians, "Be ready to give a reason for your hope."

The Blessed Mother is a big reason for hope. As Christians we always live in hope and always live with joy, because with God's grace, everything can change for the better in an instant.

So I will close with a favorite quote from that deeply devoted son of Mary, St. Josemaría:

"Heaven and earth seem to merge, my sons and daughters, on the horizon. But where they really meet is in your hearts, when you sanctify your everyday lives."[18]

Yes, Our Lady is at the crossroads of history: human history, your history, my history. And one day, God willing, she will speak up for us in the presence of Christ in heaven.

---

[18] St. Josemaría Escrivá: *Conversations with St. Josemaría Escrivá*, 116.

Some Sources

The Catholic Encyclopedia. New York: The Encyclopedia Press, Inc., 1913.

Asolt Aradi: *Shrines to Our Lady*. New York: Farrar, Straus and Young, 1954. Text at CatholicCulture.org.

Warren H. Carroll: *The Building of Christendom*. Christendom College Press, 1987.

Samuel Taylor Coleridge: "The Ancient Mariner." In W. Wordsworth, *Lyrical Ballads, with Other Poems*. London: T. Longman and O. Rees, 1800.

George W. Cox: *The Crusades*. New York: Scribner, Armstrong, and Co., 1874.

St. Josemaría Escrivá: *Conversations with Saint Josemaría Escrivá*. Strongville (Ohio): Scepter Publishers, 2011.

Richard Ford: *A Handbook for Travellers in Spain*. London: John Murray, 1882.

The Koran, translated from the Arabic by the Rev. J. M. Rodwell. London: J. M. Dent & Sons; New York: E. P. Dutton & Co., 1909.

Julius E. Olson and Edward Gaylord Bourne, editors: *The Northmen, Columbus and Cabot*. New York: Charles Scribner's Sons, 1906.

Karl August Schimmer et al.: *The Sieges of Vienna by the Turks*. Translated by the Earl of Ellesmere. London: John Murray, 1879.

Fulton J. Sheen: *The World's First Love*. San Francisco: Ignatius Press, 1996.

Robert Southey: *Roderick, the Last of the Goths*. London: Longman, Hurst, Rees, Orme, and Brown, 1818.

Thomas Aquinas: *The "Summa Theologica" of Thomas Aquinas*. Translated by Fathers of the English Dominican Province. London: R. & T. Washbourne, Ltd., 1914.

About the Author

Rev. Francis J. Hoffman ("Fr. Rocky")

Executive Director/CEO of Relevant Radio®
Board Member and Treasurer, Relevant Radio Board of Directors

Rev. Francis J. Hoffman, JCD, "Fr. Rocky," serves as Executive Director/ CEO of Relevant Radio® in addition to serving on the Board of Directors for Relevant Radio.

Since 2003, Fr. Rocky has been a regular contributor to Relevant Radio programs. He was appointed Executive Director in April, 2010.

Born and raised in suburban Chicago (Mundelein), Fr. Hoffman has been a member of Opus Dei for over 40 years. Ordained as a priest in 1992, he holds a doctorate in Canon Law from the Pontifical University of the Holy Cross, Rome, an M.B.A. from the University of Notre Dame, and a B.A. from Northwestern University in History.

Fr. Hoffman is heard on the Relevant Radio network and has appeared on other radio and television networks. Additional books written by Fr. Hoffman include 54 Day Rosary Novena, The Memorare Moment, and Marriage Insurance.

Relevant Radio brings Christ to the world through the media, broadcasting 24/7 on over 171 stations in 42 states and across the world over the internet and the free mobile app. Relevant Radio owns and operates 102 stations and produces 85 hours of original programming each week.

Relevant Radio creates a community of hope. Through this personal and intimate forum of communications, marriages are saved, souls draw closer to Christ and His Church, and the Truth sets many free.

Mission Statement

Relevant Radio brings Christ to the world through the media.

Guiding Principles

Faithful to the Magisterium and Catechism of the Catholic Church
United to the Bishops
Under the protective intercession of the Blessed Virgin Mary

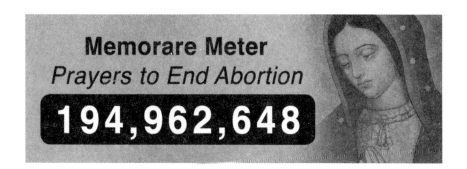

Memorare Meter
Prayers to End Abortion

194,962,648

As of February 5, 2020.

Please join Relevant Radio in praying Memorares for the end of abortion. This is a most powerful prayer, and "this kind can only be cast out by prayer and fasting." (Mt 17:20)

You can pray the Memorare yourself, or with friends, family, or with your class at school. Once you've accumulated 100 Memorares, visit www.relevantradio.com/mom so together we can track on our "Memorare Meter" and encourage others to pray more.

May God bless you and may Our Lady of Guadalupe, Protectress of the Unborn, hear our prayers!